ADVANCING THE PROFESSION OF EXERCISE PHYSIOLOGY

In recent times, the ASEP (American Society of Exercise Physiologists) leaders have developed and implemented academic standards to promote professionalism in academic programs throughout the U.S. The effort represents a significant change in the scope and the monitoring of the exercise physiologists' accountability. Through these new standards, all academic exercise physiologists are challenged by ASEP to accept responsibility for promoting the professionalization and self-regulation that will lead to improved client and patient care when prescribing exercise medicine.

Accreditation helps to reduce unnecessary variation within and between academic programs. Moreover, given the collaborative improvement in academic programs and faculty responsibility to the undergraduate students, the quality of their educational care will be significantly improved. Academic exercise physiologists must take responsibility for where exercise physiology is today and take responsibility to the evolving state of exercise physiology and student market-driven career opportunities in exercise medicine.

Advancing the Profession of Exercise Physiology provides understanding and guidance on the importance and the significance of academic leadership in promoting the profession of exercise physiology as a healthcare profession that is founded on professionalism, accreditation, ethical practice, and entrepreneurial skills.

This new volume examines the ethical need for professionalism in exercise physiology, which is, in turn, imperative for future growth and sustainability.

Tommy Boone, Ph.D., MPH, MAM, MBA, FASEP, EPC, is a founding member and first President of the American Society of Exercise Physiologists (ASEP).

ADVANCING THE PROFESSION OF EXERCISE PHYSIOLOGY

Tommy Boone

NEW YORK AND LONDON

First published 2019
by Routledge
52 Vanderbilt Avenue, New York, NY 10017

and by Routledge
2 Park Square, Milton Park, Abingdon, Oxon OX14 4RN

Routledge is an imprint of the Taylor & Francis Group, an informa business

© 2019 Taylor & Francis

The right of Tommy Boone to be identified as author of this work has been asserted by him in accordance with sections 77 and 78 of the Copyright, Designs and Patents Act 1988.

All rights reserved. No part of this book may be reprinted or reproduced or utilised in any form or by any electronic, mechanical, or other means, now known or hereafter invented, including photocopying and recording, or in any information storage or retrieval system, without permission in writing from the publishers.

Trademark notice: Product or corporate names may be trademarks or registered trademarks, and are used only for identification and explanation without intent to infringe.

Library of Congress Cataloging-in-Publication Data
Names: Boone, Tommy, author.
Title: Advancing the profession of exercise physiology / Tommy Boone.
Description: New York, NY : Routledge, 2019. |
Includes bibliographical references and index.
Identifiers: LCCN 2018045610| ISBN 9780367142841 (hardback) |
ISBN 9780367142865 (pbk.) | ISBN 9780429031144 (ebook)
Subjects: LCSH: Exercise physiologists--Professional ethics. |
Exercise--Physiological aspects.
Classification: LCC QP301 .B638 2019 | DDC 612.7/6--dc23
LC record available at https://lccn.loc.gov/2018045610

ISBN: 978-0-367-14284-1 (hbk)
ISBN: 978-0-367-14286-5 (pbk)
ISBN: 978-0-429-03114-4 (ebk)

Typeset in Bembo
by Taylor & Francis Books

CONTENTS

Foreword   *vii*
Preface   *x*
Acknowledgments   *xii*
Introduction   *xiii*

1 The Academic Challenges of Exercise Physiology   1
2 Being Open to Possibilities   12
3 Students or Research   21
4 New Leadership   31
5 We Have a Destiny to Fulfill   39
6 Courage Is Essential   46
7 The Search for Leaders   54
8 Thinking Straight   63
9 Our Destiny Is Exercise Medicine   79
10 Healthcare Provider   98
11 Transcending Our Limits   116
12 Time for a Change   124

13 Exercise Physiology and Business	130
14 The ASEP Path	136
Epilogue	145
Index	*148*

FOREWORD

Tommy Boone states that the right exercise physiology education will produce a better-version-of-ourselves. If ASEP is to thrive and fulfill its vision, it will be because exercise physiologists decided that survival means replacing their flawed sports medicine habit with a profession-specific habit. Do we want to teach our students about the profession of exercise physiology and the healthcare opportunities for Board Certified Exercise Physiologists? Or, do we want to continue graduating personal trainers? Similarly, do we want to prepare college graduates for public health service or Bob's Gym with no healthcare benefits or a sustainable financial income? Or, do we believe that by teaching them about ASEP, professionalism, ethics, standards of practice, and the EPC, they will be better prepared for life?

Given the passion for change, there is nothing in this book about imposing the ASEP views on exercise physiologists. Rather, it is about the effort to lead exercise physiologists through their confusion and misplaced reasoning to the beauty of dialogue and authentic possibilities. The hunger for truth should ignite in all of us the desire to overcome ignorance and indifference. The ASEP path is not likely to convince every exercise physiologist of the need to come together and support professionalism, but we shouldn't let what we can't do stop us from doing what we can.

If we can develop the desire in exercise physiologists to question present-day thinking and seek the truth through increased understanding of the need for their own professional organization, we will have served them rightly. But, to do this, we must stimulate within them the desire and energy to know the truth that will shape their future. Hence, wherever the moment presents itself, why not take a moment and look exercise physiologists and the students of exercise physiology in the eyes and tell them the truth?

Everyone who cares about the professionalization of exercise physiology understands the need to nurture friendships and share the ASEP story to better understand our doubts, questions, and possibilities. We need to get beyond being paralyzed by fear of what our colleagues and friends may say. In fact, unless we are willing to admit that we are not where we should be and that we have failed our students, we will not succeed. That is why Dr. Boone will not stop at finding a solution to the self-serving compromises of the failed leadership.

All professions need authentic leadership. Being a college teacher does not make a person a leader, which begs the all-important question: Where are the leaders in exercise physiology? Who speaks for the profession of exercise physiology? Just because a person with a medical degree or a physiology degree writes an exercise physiology text, does it make that person a leader in exercise physiology? Yet, that is apparently what we have witnessed and believed for decades. We need leaders who are willing to do what must be done—to move exercise physiology alongside the other healthcare professions.

Dr. Boone points out that publishing research papers is important, but so is teaching. Those who publish are moved up in academic rank, tenure, and salary. Why can't exercise physiologists do both research and teaching with the same passion and reward? Does it not strike you as sad that our own academic exercise physiologists suffer from the lack of genuine guidance and leadership? After all, the development of sincere leaders is not only the key for survival in exercise physiology, it is critical to helping the students of exercise physiology find success in the public sector.

President Harry S. Truman commented, "Men make history and not the other way around. In periods where there is no leadership, society stands still." Well, ASEP is doing what it can to get academic exercise physiologists up and moving. It is doing its best to inspire members to have confidence in developing exercise physiology as a healthcare profession.

Unfortunately, though, the indifference by many exercise physiologists to upgrade the undergraduate academic degree continues to be problematic. Those who teach at the doctorate level are frozen in the phrase, "This is how it has always been done. Why change? It works for me!" No wonder there is this huge wall of "do nothing" between right and wrong and willing and unwilling. They are afraid of changing.

I understand that not everyone will respond to the ASEP's call to change. College teachers are human. Some will change, but most will be very slow to do so. The truth is that everyone is uncomfortable with rejection and criticism, so they hold back their true feelings and ideas until that critical day when they demonstrate the courage to act. Think about it: if we allow our fear to keep us from trying, then no one would be an athlete, no one would write a poem, and no one would ask that special person for a date.

Let's face it. What we think and believe, we create. If professors are spending all their time thinking about research and writing scientific papers and are seldom, if ever, thinking about the profession of exercise physiology, there is no success in the latter.

Publishing research and doing nothing else is not true success. Professors must serve their students. Hence, even though many professors are fantastic at analyzing and discussing the biochemistry of a progressive exercise test, it is noteworthy that they are not ASEP members and they are not benefitting exercise physiology. When the faculty robs from their students, they rob from themselves.

Conversely, take a moment to think of the faculty member who completed the paper work to attend an ASEP meeting. Why did she do that knowing the Chair's commitment to sports medicine and exercise science? The answer is not complicated, at least not for the person who understands that life requires courage. Without the courage to act, you have the answer to why your talented colleague never became a great teacher. Taking control is seldom easy, but more often than not it is the right thing to do (especially in the face of indifference and criticism), and it requires a writer like Dr. Boone to bring these issues to the forefront.

Shane Paulson, MS, EPC
Board Certified Exercise Physiologist
CEO, ASEP

PREFACE

This book is published at a time when asking critical questions about the Establishment is frowned upon. Yes, doing so isn't easy for the obvious reasons pertaining to friends, colleagues, and keeping a job. Even though the reason for ASEP's existence is the promotion of professionalism in exercise physiology, one must wonder why exercise physiologists are so slow to support the change process.

The reason for another professionalism book about exercise physiology is because very little has changed since the first *Professional Development of Exercise Physiology* book by Dr. Boone was published in 2000. The academic exercise physiologists are still indifferent to the necessity for thinking as an exercise physiologist versus as a college professor. The academics of today come across as not knowing or caring about the ASEP view of exercise physiology, its leadership, our destiny, the courage to change, and importance of transcending traditional limits.

The purpose of this book is to describe the challenges and to educate the reader of the hope of a new reality of exercise physiologists. It is written for the students and teachers of exercise physiology. The goal is to empower teachers in the discussion and application of ASEP concepts and ideas with students. It assumes that the reader's desire is to achieve a certain understanding of "what is exercise physiology" and "who is an exercise physiologist"?

It is not oriented toward research publications for which are common, nor is it about sports medicine or exercise science. It promotes a vision of ideas to help understand the ASEP organization and its efforts in the professionalization of exercise physiology. This book is about the lack of leadership in academic exercise physiology, the importance of integrity, the courage to change, exercise medicine and healthcare, taking responsibility as a college teacher, college students, making a difference, the practice of exercise physiology, ethical thinking, accreditation, and board certification.

Academic exercise physiologists must take responsibility for where exercise physiology is today. They can't just continue talking and writing about VO_2 and training adaptations and not understand their responsibility to the evolving state of exercise physiology and exercise medicine. Their students need college teachers who understand the significance of leadership and the importance that established healthcare professions place on professionalism, accreditation, ethical practice, and entrepreneurial skills.

After decades of writing articles and books about exercise physiology, ethics, healthcare career opportunities, and professionalism, I feel that Dr. Boone's work is not done. This book is another major effort to integrate and promote these topics and more among exercise physiologists. Many of his past students tell me that their views of exercise physiology have changed for the better. That is what I hope this book will do for you.

Dr. Frank Wyatt
Board Certified Exercise Physiologist
Department of Athletic Training and Exercise Physiology
Midwestern State University
Wichita Falls, TX 76308

ACKNOWLEDGMENTS

This book was in the making for several years. But, it was the last several months that gave the book form. My wife said it had to be finished so that she could plan a trip to San Diego to visit our grandchildren. She also insisted on reading it before sending it to the publisher. Believe me, Brenda's comments helped to clarify the subject matter.

I wish to thank the following individuals for their review: Dr. Frank Wyatt, an exercise physiologist at Midwestern State University, for his understanding of the need for ASEP, accreditation, and board certification, Mr. Shane Paulson, a Board Certified Exercise Physiologist and CEO of ASEP, for believing in exercise physiology as a healthcare profession, and Dr. Lonnie Lowery of the University of Mount Union for staying the course with ASEP from its beginning.

Of course, I am very grateful to Routledge/Taylor & Francis Group for turning one more dream of hope into reality with the expectation of publishing with them. My perspective on the professionalization of exercise physiology is not unique. Many members of present-day healthcare professions are asking the same questions and doing their best to inspire growth and professional development.

Lastly, I must thank you, the person who is taking the time to read this book. I hope that you will also agree to participate in the change process by telling the ASEP story to your friends and colleagues.

INTRODUCTION

It is logical and right that exercise physiology professionalism is expected to undergird the public's trust in ASEP Board Certified Exercise Physiologists. Professionalism is essential for healthcare professionals and exercise physiology is a healthcare profession. And yet, professionalism in exercise physiology is seldom talked about, much less researched. The lack of interest in professionalism and the students' welfare in and after college is as bad as medical doctors who disregard medical professionalism by failing to help maintain the health and well-being of their patients.

Just as it is necessary for medical doctors to be responsible to the needs of their patients, being responsive to the students' career needs is also central to the ethical duty of academic exercise physiologists, even if they believe they are doing everything possible for their students. After all, they are already giving up 6 hrs a week of their research time to teaching two classes.

Exercise physiology is a vocation in which an exercise physiologist's specialized knowledge and laboratory skills are put in the service of safely prescribing exercise medicine to restore and promote health and well-being.

Hence, if students are having trouble locating jobs after college, it must be the students' fault. Well, if that is how you feel, ask yourself this question: "Is the typical exercise physiology professor research-centered or teacher-centered?" Here, I should say that if the unspoken reality of academic exercise physiology is all about research and publishing and little else, it should be obvious that teaching is not considered a high priority.

The ASEP leaders' point of view is that academic exercise physiologists should redefine their work from just a research emphasis to a combination of research and student-centered professionalism. This thinking is not that crazy at all. It is what the students' parents think is already the case. That is why they send their sons and daughters to college. It is why they either pay thousands of dollars for the college tuition fees or help in giving money towards college costs.

Regardless of which path you choose (i.e., research or teach), there is a cost involved. Why not be willing to do both?

Parents are not aware of the dynamics that drive faculty discussions. They are not aware that college teachers are under great pressure to publish while teaching is an assumed activity. It is also believed the exercise physiology position is in actuality an academic discipline of researchers. Hence, although the students' ability to arrive at complex decisions should be at the heart of the students' education, the same thinking does not exist with the so-called "teachers." They learned in doctorate school that getting more publications is more important than teaching.

The notion that exercise physiology is a vocation in which the exercise physiologist's knowledge, hands-on laboratory skills, and judgment are put in the service of protecting and restoring human well-being by safely prescribing exercise medicine isn't as important. Yet, exercise physiologists are the logical 21st century healthcare professionals to administer exercise medicine in the prevention and treatment of chronic diseases and disabilities. Therefore, the students of exercise physiology must have access to credible and caring teachers that understand the need for a more rigorous concept of validating exercise physiology as a client- and/or patient-centered healthcare profession.

> *Key Point:* Teaching professionalism in exercise physiology is not only a daunting challenge, but also an opportunity to engage our occupation and teach how exercise physiologists make a living while controlling their own work.

The ASEP exercise physiologists believe it is past time to talk and write about the importance of a unified force to move academic exercise physiologists' state of mind regarding professionalism from its infancy to maturity. This statement is not the opportunity to speak badly of college teachers. It is the effort of the ASEP exercise physiologists to influence the non-ASEP exercise physiologists to promote student-centered professionalism.

> The unprofessional relationship of the exercise physiologists with an interest in sports nutrition and the sports supplement industry is a major challenge to exercise physiology professionalism.

ASEP leaders have developed and implemented academic standards to promote professionalism in academic programs throughout the United States. The effort represents a significant change in the scope and monitoring of the exercise physiologist's accountability. All academic exercise physiologists are challenged by ASEP to accept responsibility for promoting the professionalization and self-regulation that will lead to improved client and patient care when prescribing exercise medicine. Accreditation helps to reduce unnecessary variation within and between academic programs. Also, given the collaborative improvement in academic programs and faculty responsibility to the undergraduate students, the quality of their educational care will be significantly improved.

While the challenge of achieving the new ASEP configuration of accredited academic exercise physiology programs is daunting, given that it will run counter to the existing *status quo,* it is absolutely imperative that it is done. Professional standards are symbolic of the academic common-sense efforts to increase self-regulation that benefits the members of the profession. This is important for a number of reasons. In particular, it helps students and their parents select academic programs that will provide the educational preparation and hands-on experience to be successful as healthcare professionals.

Accreditation will also help to ensure that the curriculum is credible and conforms to the expectations of the ASEP scientific knowledge and practice of the profession. Unaccredited programs will leave exercise physiology students with a degree that is worthless for getting a job after college. Also, it is logical that such programs make it difficult for students to obtain ASEP certification due to the poor educational standards.

Exercise physiology professionalism should be promoted, developed, and taught in the academic curriculum at the undergraduate and postgraduate training levels.

Thus, the following question needs an answer so that everyone will know what is what. "Is the practice of exercise physiology a science, a trade, a business, or a combination of one or more?" As far as I believe and as I have stated many times in the *Professionalization of Exercise Physiology-online* and the *Journal of Professional Exercise Physiology* electronic journals, exercise physiology is a healthcare profession based on scientific knowledge and specialized hands-on experiences. Hence, as a profession, exercise physiology is based on selfless and compassionate service for all students, clients, and patients.

Unfortunately, the problem is that at present there are no academic courses that address professionalism in exercise physiology. The academic exercise physiologists are not interested in teaching a course on the professional development of exercise physiology. They do not want restrictions of any kind, particularly regarding their financial relationship with sports supplement companies.

Far too often academic exercise physiologists interested in sports nutrition and the grants they get to promote supplements to unfairly enhance athletic performance are increasing. As they say, "money talks." Throw some major bucks toward the academic setting and essentially everyone will stop in their tracks. The mission entrusted to college teachers has changed from a highly ethical, academic-oriented student caring approach to education to "what's in for me" mentality.

It is true that academic institutions have problems that society and college teachers are not aware of at this moment in history. These problems are not going to simply disappear. They have been with us for decades, and they are only going to get worse without exercise physiology leadership. For now, I see them as opportunities to change, grow, and become more effective as college teachers. I see the challenges of our age as a chance for exercise physiologists to envision once again what it truly means to take the step towards something better. And so, as a member of ASEP, I need to ask: "Is sports medicine or exercise science the equivalent of an academic degree in exercise physiology?" If it isn't, which is the truth, why are exercise physiologists on their knees before non-exercise physiologists?

Tommy Boone, Ph.D., MPH, MAM, MBA
Board Certified Exercise Physiologist

1

THE ACADEMIC CHALLENGES OF EXERCISE PHYSIOLOGY

An academic exercise physiologist would probably tell you that exercise physiology is all about athletics and research. But, the question is this: Is it true? Or, is exercise physiology more about exercise medicine and healthcare? If the latter is true, this means recent college graduates are more likely to find employment.

It is frustrating to read that a college teacher (1) with a doctorate and master's degree in Exercise Science (who teaches in a Kinesiology Department) said, "Exercise physiology is a sub-discipline of kinesiology that addresses the short-term biological responses to the stress of physical activity and how the body adapts to repeated bouts of physical activity over time ...." While there is nothing new about what he said, it is strangely uncomfortable to think that just anyone believes he or she is an authority in defining exercise physiology? It is not only questionable to share misinformation, it is wrong as well. The problem is so many faculty members work in such an isolated academic subculture that they have distorted the view of "what is exercise physiology."

> Exercise physiology is NOT just the study of the acute responses and chronic adaptations to a wide range of exercise conditions.

Coincidentally, it is amazing that such misinformation still exists 20 years after the founding of ASEP, the American Society of Exercise Physiologists. Located on the ASEP website is the correct definition (2). It says that Exercise Physiology is

> The comprehensive delivery of treatment services concerned with the analysis, improvement, and maintenance of the physiological mechanisms underlying physical and mental health and fitness through regular exercise, the prevention

and/or treatment of chronic diseases and/or disabilities with exercise medicine, and the professional guidance of athletes and others interested in athletics and sports training.

It is embarrassing to address the failed thinking that undergirds exercise science and related academic degree programs. As time has passed, I have gained a perspective on "what is exercise physiology" and its far-reaching healthcare implications. It is clear that many college professors are scared to challenge the status quo. And yet, the empty rhetoric and hypocrisy covered in the hierarchy of academic research does not pass the smell test due to the faculty's failure to adhere to an ethical emphasis on teaching.

Cynics may sneer, but a brief assessment of the definition of kinesiology is misleading. It does not say anything that links kinesiology to a specific career after graduation. For example, the American Kinesiology Association (AKA) statement (3) says,

> It includes, but is not limited to, such areas of study as exercise science, sports management, athletic training and sports medicine, socio-cultural analyses of sports, sport and exercise psychology, fitness leadership, physical education-teacher education, and pre-professional training for physical therapy, occupational therapy, medicine and other health related fields.

> A very important objective of ASEP is to set the agenda, enhance, and increase visibility of exercise physiology as a healthcare profession.

Conversely, ASEP describes exercise physiology as a healthcare profession:

> ... the comprehensive delivery of treatment services concerned with the analysis, improvement, and maintenance of the physiological mechanisms underlying physical and mental health and fitness through regular exercise, the prevention and/or treatment of chronic diseases and/or disabilities with exercise medicine ....

Board Certified Exercise Physiologists

The ASEP Board Certified Exercise Physiologists are healthcare professionals with an academic degree in exercise physiology. They have passed the Exercise Physiologist Certified (EPC) exam and, therefore, are certified to practice exercise physiology (2). Establishing and implementing standards of practice are major functions of a professional organization. The purpose of the ASEP standards is to describe the professional ethic and responsibilities for which Board Certified Exercise Physiologists are accountable.

The purpose of the Exercise Physiology Practice is to describe the specific responsibilities for which exercise physiologists are accountable. The ASEP "Standards" comprise four areas: promoting health and wellness; preventing illness and disability; restoring health; and helping athletes reach their potential in sports training and performance. Implicit with the ASEP organization is the point of view that exercise physiology is a healthcare profession. They are not personal trainers. ASEP is not a fitness instructor organization.

Epidemiologic evidence supports the healthcare benefits of regular exercise in the development and maintenance of health and well-being (4). Now, with the ASEP Board Certification as the gold standard for exercise physiologists in the United States, the supervision, safety, and care of clients and/or patients will increasingly become more evident throughout the public sector.

Certified Exercise Physiologists are trained to: (a) administer exercise stress tests in healthy and unhealthy populations; (b) evaluate a person's health, with special attention to cardiovascular function and metabolism; (c) develop individualized exercise prescriptions to increase physical fitness and muscle strength, endurance, and flexibility; (d) design customized exercise programs to decrease the increase in risk associated with existing adverse health conditions due to physical inactivity; and (e) meet the needs of athletes of all ages and their athletic performance goals (3).

Exercise physiologists play a very important role in today's healthcare. Exercise is medical treatment, and exercise medicine is often equal to if not more effective than the prescription of certain medicines (4). Even low intensity exercise medicine (such as brisk walking) helps to provide protection for individuals at risk of developing heart disease, high blood pressure, and type 2 diabetes mellitus.

> The failure of the highest-level exercise physiologists to understand the needs of their colleagues who are at a lower level of academic development is a problem.

While our first impulse may be to turn a blind eye to exercise as medicine, Courtney Kipps (5) said, "Exercise is an extraordinarily effective prescription to combat chronic disease, perhaps the most effective." No doubt this is why a greater number of medical doctors are referring their patients to ASEP Board Certified Exercise Physiologists. After all, they have the educational training and laboratory skills to teach their clients and/or patients how to benefit from a personalized exercise medicine program that is progressive, sound, and safe (6).

The exercise physiology degree provides college graduates with the academic education and hands-on skills to help individuals with low back pain, osteoarthritis, cardiovascular disease, high blood pressure, musculoskeletal disabilities, and obesity. Thus, the profession of exercise physiology is similar to the physical therapy profession in that it also provides services that relieve pain, restore function, and prevent or limit permanent physical disabilities (7). Both professions teach clients and patients how to achieve an increase in their quality of life. Now, with the ASEP Board Certification as the gold standard for exercise physiologists, the supervision, safety, and care of clients and patients are increasingly evident in caring for the health of the public sector.

In addition, Board Certified Exercise Physiologists work with older and aging clients and patients to help prevent loss of mobility before it occurs by developing safe fitness and wellness programs for a healthier and more active lifestyle. They perform healthcare functions in a variety of settings that include hospitals, private practices, outpatient health and fitness clinics, home health agencies, schools, sports and fitness facilities, work settings, and nursing and assisted living homes (8). Their professional practice also includes consulting, research, and educational services for which they are held accountable to the ASEP Code of Ethics (9) and ASEP Standards of Professional Practice (10).

Failure of Academic Leadership

Unfortunately, the decline in ethical thinking within the American colleges and universities has allowed for the continuation of meaningless academic degree programs. While every academic degree should be driven by a purpose, it doesn't take much to realize that is not the case. If you were to disagree, ask yourself "What is the purpose of going to college?" Is it to say that I have a college degree and that is it? Or, is it to get a financially good job after college? I believe the latter is the reason why students and their parents pay the high tuition fees to attend college classes. They want to get a great job and move on with their lives. They want to be able to financially support themselves after college (11).

Otherwise, the alternative is to graduate from college and move back home. Did you know that 1 out every 2 college graduates between 18 and 24 years of age is living at home with their parents? As I see it, finding yourself unemployed after college means the college degree is meaningless. If I am right, what responsibility do the college teachers, chairs, deans, vice-presidents, presidents, and others have in marketing academic degrees that do not help students be successful in life after college? Where is the administrative and faculty leadership to help ensure that the integrity of academic institutions?

As the Chair of the Department of Exercise Physiology for 16 years at The College of St. Scholastica in Duluth, MN, I had parents say to me that, "College administrators are a major part of the students' problem if not 'the' problem why recent college graduates are living at home." They would then ask me the question, "Do the professors here at St. Scholastica realize they have responsibilities to their students, such as being prepared to teach and being truthful about the academic degree?" My answer was always,

> Yes, each of the four faculty members in this department understands his role in preparing students for success as a healthcare provider. That is why I

changed the degree title from exercise science to exercise physiology after assuming the chair position. That is also why I founded the American Society of Exercise Physiologists in 1997 to lay the professional foundation for success as healthcare professionals after graduating from college.

Getting an academic degree is more than attending classes, making friends, and going to athletic events. Yet, the administration and faculty seem to think that is good enough. Degree programs must be updated and carefully linked to responsible employment after college. After all, the parents are often paying the tuition and living costs not to mention providing a car while paying the notes and insurance if not the gas to and from college plus spending money.

While it seems reasonable that the academic administrators and faculty understand why an academic major should be designed to facilitate getting a job, their thinking is apparently driven by the shared desire to protect their jobs at all costs. This means they are committed to the common cause of sustaining status quo, which is doing whatever is necessary to increase tuition costs. In support of this point, the long-term trend for college tuition has been rising almost 6% above the rate of inflation. Clearly, groupthink thrives in colleges and universities as well as in the business world (12).

Students and families every year are forced deeper into debt to get a degree that they were led to believe would help locate a financially good job. And yet, directors, department chairs, and faculty understand they have done essentially nothing to plan for the students' success. Meantime, physical therapists, athletic trainers, nurses, occupational therapists, and physician assistants understand the importance of professionalism, standards of professional practice, and the need for excellent career opportunities. They are successful at promoting their students and the vision of their individual professions.

Many academic exercise physiologists do not support the ASEP vision (13) or the ASEP professional organization. This is disappointing for all the obvious reasons, particularly from a professional development point of view. Just as physical therapy healthcare professionals understand the need to come together, exercise physiologists must do the same and support a common professional and ethical agenda. But, this isn't the case at the present time because too many exercise physiologists think of themselves as "physiologists" even though they do not have a degree in physiology.

Publishing research articles has trumped any discussion of professionalism. No doubt it is their means to feeling better about their work and themselves. Another reason for not supporting the ASEP organization is because the college teachers were not taught to think as healthcare professionals (14) or that teaching is at least equal to doing research. But, once again, they are unaware of the emotional needs of students and they are not able to give students what they need. They do not understand professionalism and so it is natural for them to not place the students' needs above their own needs.

Although it is correct to conclude that consumer dissatisfaction (particularly the parents of exercise science students), has not reached a peak at the department level yet, it will and when it does it will produce important changes. Criticisms, in particular, will be specific to the out-dated purpose of the departments' agenda across the United States and the failure of the faculty to update degree plans to make them relevant. It is also logical (just as it is taking place with PE classes in high schools throughout the U.S.) that the mix of kinesiology, exercise science, human performance, and other similar, non-professional academic majors will be decreased if not deleted from the list of academic degrees.

No doubt some faculty members understand these points but fear for their jobs should they speak up. After all, approximately 50% of the college and university faculty consists of adjunct faculty. Even tenured faculty members realize that tenure no longer protection when sharing the truth with their colleagues, especially if it highlights the failure in academic and/or administrative leadership. However, it reasonable to say that no academic department or institution will be successful for long if either is isolated from the students' reality of expecting a credible job after college.

Working at Bob's Gym for $12–$15 per hour without health insurance is not sufficient to pay the $30,000 or a $130,000 tuition debt after graduation (11). In time, parents will be asking the Chairperson, Dean, or Vice-President, "What are your employability strategies for our sons and daughters?" The bottom line is this: If there are no strategies, then, not knowing and/or not doing what is right is the wrong behavior for academic administrators with high salaries. They must have the backbone to do everything possible to provide their graduates the best opportunity of gaining credible employment.

The academic institution's apparent lack of responsibility to the students is causing parents to ask the question, "Where is the administrators' responsibility to the students?" Others are asking, "Why are the colleges and universities charging increasingly higher tuition fees and living costs for an academic degree that does not address legitimate needs and standards of society?"

Moreover, where are the college teachers who should be teaching about professionalism in exercise physiology, an EP-specific code of ethics, board certification, standards of practice, business skills, and entrepreneurship (15)? Here again, it is clear that the exercise physiologists are not loyal or committed to their students' needs.

Students, alumni, university administrators, and parents need answers to these questions, and they need them today not decades from now. No parents should encourage or financially help their children major in exercise science or any academic major that is not designed for the college graduate to enter a career-specific job. Yes, understandably, this is a bold statement, but it is the conclusion reached by many parents I have talked with during my 40+ years of college teaching.

Not surprisingly, when recent college graduates return home earlier than their parents had expected, there is a problem. Either they were not able to think through critically important ideas, understand issues, meet the employers' expectations, or they were seduced into thinking they would locate a credible job when they graduate when such jobs do not exist. Yet, it is clear that without professional leadership, new thinking and training and, very importantly, changes at the department level, nothing in academia will get better and the students will stay jobless.

Also, as long as college professors fail to get involved in promoting the professionalism in exercise physiology, the parents will feel they were robbed of the college tuition they paid to the respective academic institutions to help their sons and daughters earn a college degree. In fact, many parents and their college-age students are wondering just how much higher the tuition will rise before graduation.

WHERE IS THE INTEGRITY?

Parents from all across the United States believed that they were getting honest feedback from academic advisors and college representatives, but this is rarely true. In fact, many parents and some college teachers have come to think of this common belief as a myth that is consistent with the purposeful intent of employees to avoid "speaking the truth" for a variety of reasons—mostly, to protect their jobs. This is worth repeating, especially since it is so pernicious. Share these thoughts with your friends and family.

Consumer dissatisfaction is the first step to addressing the problem of unethical academic settings. Higher education must be reformed and updated if it is going to benefit the public. People with integrity must get into the driver's seat. College administrators and faculty members must be held accountable for their actions. In particular, significant reform is required of the exercise science programs that are in reality one or two courses away from the physical education curriculum of the 1960s.

Interestingly, with respect to the physical education degree, at least it is reasonable to conclude that the students earn a degree linked to a teaching and coaching career. This is not the case with the exercise science students. Why the faculty of these programs do not get that the exercise science degree and, similarly, the kinesiology, sport science, and human performance degrees are largely undifferentiated in the eyes of the public is a mystery. All anyone can say is that it must result from a strong status quo driven by the faculty's interest independent of their responsibility as teachers to provide students with core competencies and career-specific knowledge. Also, the pressures of groupthink are powerful, which is exactly why they refuse to think outside the norms.

The behavior of the exercise physiology faculty devalues college teaching since the students are not provided with the best chance of gaining employment. And yet, society is dependent on academic institutions to educate and prepare young men and women for employment. It is an even bigger problem when the chairs, deans, and vice-presidents who do not understand that they are also responsible for the high rates of bachelor-level unemployment. They should be supporting the students by ensuring that the degree programs make sense and are a good investment.

If the degree programs are not a good investment, they are worthless. This means they should either be updated or deleted from the institution's academic majors. With regard to exercise science, working the system and putting one's own interests ahead of the students are unacceptable. The degree title and curriculum should be updated to exercise physiology from which the chairperson and the faculty should step up to the plate and do everything that is necessary to create a career-specific academic major, which will be much better than setting a publishing record in the department.

The college system and its employees must wake up and begin to demand fiscal accountability so that future generations will have the ability to experience the "American Dream." Character is more important than gaming the system. It is not an easy path to travel, but it is possible, and it is necessary. In part, this means moving beyond encouraging exercise physiology students to think of themselves as exercise specialists, personal trainers, fitness instructors, and exercise professionals. After all, with a degree in exercise physiology, the students will graduate as exercise physiologists.

From the ASEP perspective, it is also important that the degree is ASEP accredited (16) and the students sit for the ASEP Board Certification. The professors should refer to their past students as ASEP Board Certified Exercise Physiologists. This means the faculty realizes that self-respect is more important than publishing another research paper.

This transformation from yesterday's narcissistic focus on more research gives way to connecting the essence of the exercise physiology degree with a healthcare profession, such as working as an entrepreneur in exercise medicine (17). Taken a step further, it means that the professors must teach their students with the understanding they are to become practicing members of the healthcare profession.

This perspective is important because students have said that they are tired of professors and department Chairs' inattentive behavior to their need to think critically, to solve problems, and to speak and write cogently, particularly when it comes to professionalism, ethical behavior, and standards of practice. They have said that the teachers' neglect of embracing and promoting ASEP and its vision for all exercise physiologists isn't just wrong, it is selfish and dysfunctional.

To be frank, after many years of working with college teachers who were not in the least bit interested, much less committed, to the academic development and/or the mentoring of their students, it was unsettling and difficult. In practice they were taught that the doctorate degree meant they could spend most of their academic time publishing research papers and building their resumes. The act of teaching was little more than a necessary requirement that was tolerated. Teaching was not their passion and they did not have the commitment to help much less empower students beyond general expectations. Even working with colleagues in the same department was looked upon as a required necessity with neither an interest nor the pursuit of a common cause.

Final Thoughts

Throughout the history of the healthcare professions (such as nursing, physical therapy, occupational therapy, and athletic training), there has never been a shortage of men and women willing to do what they believed was necessary to promote their profession. They were then and still are engaged in writing, talking, and living the path they understood to be successful. This type of academia contributes to the increased equality between those with a job (professors) and the students who anticipate locating credible career opportunities.

Where are the caring professors? Where are the authentic exercise physiology leaders? Where are the academic exercise physiologists interested in students more than their tenure and research? Where are the professors who are focused on helping students get ready for the world after college?

The answer to each question is the same. For the most part they do not exist. College professors are interested in publishing research papers and that is it. Teaching is left to the adjunct faculty. Deception governs everything in academia. It is the accepted norm, which is also the case with the large lecture classes that are needed to retain students to make the budget. Integrity and college teaching are things of the past. In theory, it sounds good but the two do not exist. Thus, the students' education limps along far behind the vision of a traditional education. In truth, colleges are doing little more than loading the students up with debt they cannot pay off in the unemployment line.

While some teachers are restless with business-as-usual, the notion of being faithful to the teaching profession and empowering students is buried beneath the mediocrity or worse (i.e., the lack of accountability). The passion for serving students and society's health concerns hardly exist and for certain seldom talked about. This is true for students who graduate from public colleges and those who were accepted in private institutions. This is a harsh reality that needs to be faced.

The not-so-obvious lack of support for profession-specific jobs and career-specific opportunities in exercise physiology is creating hopelessness in the lives of students. And, to make problems worst, it exists in the midst of large tuition loans and disappointment with academic system. The students' concerns are unmistakably clear and real.

They are saying, "Step up to the plate academic EPs and do something about this mess we find ourselves in when we graduate." Their plea is reinforced by their parents' dissatisfaction with the college advisors, department chairs and their faculty, and the Deans who could require the academic exercise physiologists to get with the program. Meantime, the students are disillusioned and searching for answers.

College teachers cannot enhance the public's perception and/or view of them by not placing a high priority on teaching. They do not raise the professors' status in society engaging predominantly in activities that benefit them with little hope of helping students. College teachers can't just work for themselves. Teaching is a public service even if it is not recognized as such by the colleges and universities. Should you disagree, be honest with yourself and admit it while being open to the purpose of getting a college degree.

It is believed that an authentic education is linked to a person's purpose in life. But, this can only be true if the education is meaningful. Unfortunately, though, the greatest problem of academia in our age is the faculty's need to think that their job is "all about them." After all, professors spent a lot time completing the doctorate degree so why shouldn't they believe the academic position is their playground for a life time of reward in return. The true feelings for most of them are that the needs of their students are not more important than their own personal needs.

However, there is a better path. It is one that leads to better teachers and caring human beings. It is not a secret or self-righteous path. For many decades, members of other professions have walked this path. The "professionalism" path is not without its ups and downs but it is the right journey to take. Above all else, it is important that academic exercise physiologists rise to the occasion to make this journey. Remember, it's never too late to change. Do not worry or despair when disagreements become commonplace. Check your motivation and stay true to ending "what is" for "what should be."

The purpose of promoting professionalism in exercise physiology is the same never-ending work that physical therapists and others do. It must be constantly pursued, celebrated, and applied in our thoughts with written and spoken words and actions. When all is said and done the commitment to teaching is what counts. The challenge is for all exercise physiologists to open their minds to "what is exercise physiology" and the role and necessity of new ideas and the significance of professionalism and entrepreneurship.

> Accountability is imperative. Faculty members with integrity understand this point. They know it is important to share intelligible and transparent facts and information with students and their parents. They understand the ASEP point of view, especially when it comes to the differences between the fitness instructor and the Board Certified Exercise Physiologist. They know that ASEP is the professional organization for exercise physiologists just as the APTA is the professional organization for physical therapists.

Once the academic exercise physiologists actually accept who they are and what they do, they will come to understand their destiny. They will stop doing things that bring forth failure and dissatisfaction to their students. They will start work on behalf of building their own profession of exercise physiology.

Therefore, all exercise physiologists must become ASEP members and support the organization's effort to promote the professionalization of exercise physiology. Exercise physiologists and the healthcare community should come together with the understanding that exercise medicine takes its roots in exercise physiology.

References

1 Davis, P. (2015). What Is Exercise Physiology? (Online). www.quora.com/What-is-the-definition-of-exercise-physiology.
2 American Society of Exercise Physiologists. (2017). What is Exercise Physiology? (Online). www.asep.org/about-asep/definition/.
3 American Kinesiology Association. (2018). Definition of Kinesiology. (Online). http://americankinesiology.org/SubPages/Pages/About.
4 Explore Health Careers. (2017). Exercise Physiologist. (Online). http://explorehealthcareers.org/en/career/142/exercise_physiologist#Tab=overview.
5 Kipps, C. (2010). International Perspectives on Exercise Medicine: Exercise in the Prevention and Treatment of Chronic Disease. (Online). www.wcmt.org.uk/sites/default/files/migrated-reports/794_1.pdf.
6 Brown, S. (2017). Undergraduate Programs. (Online). www.kinesiology.msstate.edu/undergraduate/.
7 Boone, T. (2015). Exercise Science Students: What Are They Owed? *Professionalization of Exercise Physiology-online*. 18;2:1–7.
8 Boone, T. (2015). A New Healthcare Profession: Exercise Physiology. *Professionalization of Exercise Physiology-online*. 18;3:1–12.
9 Boone, T. (2014). *Promoting Professionalism in Exercise Physiology*. Lewiston, NY: The Edwin Mellen Press.
10 American Society of Exercise Physiologists. (2017). Code of Ethics. (Online). www.asep.org/index.php/organization/code-ethics/.
11 American Society of Exercise Physiologists. (2017). Standards of Practice. (Online). www.asep.org/index.php/organization/practice/.
12 Boone, T. (2012). The Neglected Students of the Exercise "Applied" Sciences. *Professionalization of Exercise Physiology-online*. 15;6:1–23.
13 American Society of Exercise Physiologists. (2017). The ASEP Vision. (Online). www.asep.org/index.php/about-asep/.
14 Boone, T. (2008). The Path of Professionalism. *Professionalization of Exercise Physiology-online*. 11;9:1–14.
15 Boone, T. (2009). *The Professionalization of Exercise Physiology: Certification, Accreditation, and Standards of Practice of the American Society of Exercise Physiologists (ASEP)*. Lewiston, NY: The Edwin Mellen Press.
16 American Society of Exercise Physiologists. (2017). ASEP Accreditation. (Online). www.asep.org/index.php/professional-services/accreditation/.
17 Boone, T. (2016). *ASEP's Exercise Medicine Text for Exercise Physiologists*. Beijing, China: Bentham Science Publishing.

2

BEING OPEN TO POSSIBILITIES

Academic exercise physiologists must not let their ego get in the way of doing the right thing for their students. Thus, they must be patient, diligent, and willing to work hard on behalf of the members of the exercise physiology profession.

Being open to new ideas is critical in sharing the work that must be done to move exercise physiology into the 21st century. It is not impossible to think of exercise physiology as a profession rather than a discipline. While you may be just starting college, others may have graduated. Some may be working as exercise physiologists. If it is the latter either by carefully planned decisions or by strange events that fell into place, thinking and working as an exercise physiologist are not easy.

Exercise physiology, as I see it, is the hope of something better for our students. Is it the same for you? No doubt if you are an exercise physiologist, you are probably not very happy with the lack of state and federal agencies in regulating the practice of exercise physiology. Licensure is important, but it isn't the answer to the exercise physiologist's peace of mind and security. Rather, the answer lies in looking for creating opportunities, so you can live the life you dreamed of as a college freshman.

For many years as an exercise physiologist and healthcare professional, more than once I have questioned what I was told by other exercise physiologists (1). It isn't easy when getting out of our comfort zone, but it is your choice to think for yourself or be led by others. You can either draw closer to them if you feel the need to do so or you can live by the scripture that tells you it is possible to do all things through Christ who strengthens you (Philippians 4:13 NIV). This is important to remember, especially if you are teaching at the college level. Some of your colleagues will give you the impression they are your close personal friends, that is, until they can figure out how to get what you have. All you can do and should do is forgive and move on.

Understandably, I should also point out that I made some really good friends with colleagues who inspired me. They were uplifting and dynamic, and their love for teaching moved them to rethink their college work as an exercise physiologist.

In short, life goes on, so cultivate the mindset you need in order to grow as a college "teacher." This means putting away the bad times and making the decision to be happy and successful. Of course, it isn't always that simple, but it is a requirement if you are going to deal with the mental and emotional challenges of being open to possibilities.

Talking About Possibilities

Strangely enough, given that a college education is supposed to be about critical thinking, analytic reasoning, and encouraging new ideas, changing status quo isn't an easy possibility. Most faculty members are comfortable in the traditional academic setting. They are not aware of the possibility that it could be different. Also, it is common knowledge that very few professors who teach in a doctorate program talked about change or possibility thinking, especially the idea that exercise physiologists should support their own professional organization.

Unfortunately, as a result, there is little if any opportunity to talk about new ideas, new academic courses, new degree titles, professionalism, academic accreditation, and career expectations. It is as though the transition from health and physical education to exercise science gave way to silence for fear that the "faculty of accredited degree programs" might speak the truth about athletics and exercise science.

> Publishing research articles has overtaken our discussions with students, our colleagues, and our academic programs. It is to the point of concluding that the students' education is becoming more and more a race between higher and higher tuition loans and a catastrophe.

The primary transition from health and PE took place in the 1960s and 1970s but without an academic plan to educate students as healthcare providers. That thinking happened much later. What the physical educators understood was that faculty members who published research papers were looked at differently from the non-researchers. Also, regardless of the title of their academic degree, if they published research articles and stood in front of a metabolic analyzer to measure oxygen uptake, more often than not they referred to themselves as "exercise scientists." As strange as this thinking might sound, it is still true today. It was (and still is) the wrong option driven by a lack of leadership.

Although the secret is out, the question is this: "Is anyone listening?" No! If you don't believe me, think about it for a moment. The next time you bump into an exercise scientist, exercise physiologist, biologist, or psychologist on campus, ask this question, "How are you doing?" You are likely to get a smile if he or she has just published a research article. Then again, he or she may say very little—as is true of many members of the faculty who are overwhelmed by yesterday's rhetoric while trying to experience a new way to think and/or feel about his or her career.

It is not impossible to experience the ASEP "new way to think." In fact, it is important that exercise physiologists manage their thinking when under pressure. Occasionally, you will hit the jackpot and bump into such a person who says, "Honestly, it really isn't about the research or even the emphasis on research regardless of what everyone says. As a professor I am more interested in teaching and helping students find a credible career when they graduate."

The Teacher's Responsibility

As the administration and faculty will tell you, publishing research is talked about as being the major part of the responsibility of all college teachers. Publishing research articles is critical to getting tenure. The reward for being a "college researcher" is the acceptance by the administration and peers even if they don't like you and, often times, this is true regardless of the depth of the research. Hence, if you do not publish, you are on the outside looking in. When you do not publish more manuscripts year after year, you get a sense of being less important and/or valued by the administration.

As members of the faculty, exercise physiologists learn rather quickly there is often no one on campus to share thoughts about updating academic course work, to talk about the purpose of the department, or why the title of an academic major should be changed. And yet, it is important that academic exercise physiologists recognize their responsibility to make an original imprint that is true to their values, such as promoting professionalism in exercise physiology. They must stop being slow to talk about and debate "what is exercise physiology" and "who is an exercise physiologist" among their colleagues. The answers are obvious or should be to any college teacher with his or her eyes and heart open to helping students achieve success in landing a credible job.

Students' success depends on significant gains in learning how to think and reason, especially with regard to being prepared for the workforce. Unfortunately, though, without an emphasis on the professionalization of exercise physiology, the faculty is failing to prepare job-ready candidates. That is why most exercise science degree programs are designed to refer students to graduate programs in physical therapy, nursing, and athletic training. Academic physical therapists love it. They don't want the exercise science major to become exercise physiology because they know there would be increased competition for the leadership role in prescribing exercise medicine.

Students who major in exercise science are more often than not distressed when they realized their degree is linked to jobs that make paying back tuition loans very difficult. It does not matter two hoots that the exercise physiologists and other faculty members are publishing research articles in the exercise science department. The students are on the short end of the stick. You can rest assured their future is down and out while the nursing student graduates into a hospital job rather quickly. Also, it is clear that you can be a great researcher, but unable to see what is going on around you because you don't actually work for the students. Apparently, having a Ph.D. degree does not mean that the faculty actually cares about teaching or the students for that matter.

The greatest psychological "sell out" committed by academic exercise physiologists as college teachers is to think the academic job is their playground for raises, promotion, and recognition. First of all, while this thinking is common among all college teachers, it is an ethical failure at its highest level. Second, it is an obsession that must be corrected. The idea of gaining power and influence at the expense of the students' welfare and money, particularly, that of their parents is simply wrong. Needless to say, the academic exercise physiologists fail to get this point. Apparently, it does not enter their minds or that of the administrators.

Publishing research should not be what a college career is about, yet the faculty members understand they must double down on their research efforts year after year to survive within the educational system. Unfortunately, the world is full of misguided thinkers, including college administrators. If this is difficult to believe, take a moment and think about it. A college education should be about quality teaching, which is helping young minds grow and mature into possibilities and opportunities. It should not be about fulfilling the desires of the faculty or the growth of the department, and it should not be about the institution's financial standing or appearance with other colleges and universities.

Education, not publishing and/or accessing personal reward (e.g., promotion and/or tenure), must be the motivating force that inspires college teachers. Hence, if you are new at your academic position, be sure that you are not motivated by the "what is in it for me mentality." Regardless of the intense pressure to publish, you can be better, and you can learn to think differently. Admittedly, it isn't going to be easy. It will take courage and discipline. Above all, it will take faith in the idea that there are better reasons for being a college professor.

Failure to Pull Your Own Strings

The ASEP leadership understands the failure of academic exercise physiologists to support professionalism in exercise physiology (2). They have written a great deal about professionalism, board certification, and accreditation and, yes, pulling your own strings throughout the ASEP journals and books. Everything they have written comes back to the point that every exercise physiologist must learn to think for themselves. They understand strong peer-to-peer interaction is essential to developing trust among exercise physiologists.

So, why not decide today to pull your own strings and embrace the ASEP entrepreneur approach to healthcare? If you are an exercise physiologist, you are the key professional with the academic integrity to prescribe exercise medicine. This is a simple and powerful message. You can start your own exercise medicine clinic to prevent and treat chronic disease, but you must have the desire to develop it from within yourself.

Think of the time wasted if you allow yourself to stay plugged in to the way exercise physiologists presently think. No doubt many want to get beyond the dogma of "this is the way it has always been, so why change," but are reluctant to do so. How do I know? Because it is a common everyday expression among college teachers, and yet they refuse to examine why the present-day view of exercise physiology is problematic. Either they are comfortable with the way things are or they do not want to get on the bad side of their colleagues. Hence, due to the pressure to publish-or-perish, the non-tenured faculty members play it safe.

Mentally failing to work together on behalf of exercise physiology is the primary reason why many academic exercise physiologists are active members of generic organizations? In particular, it is believed that the American College of Sports Medicine (ACSM) is the organization to belong to. It is an excellent organization of old and new faculty with the focus on the professor-as-researcher. ACSM is a sports medicine and exercise science organization. This is an essential understanding, given that it is not an exercise physiology organization.

Sadly, most exercise physiologists are not interested in talking or thinking about the relationship between integrity and organizational performance. Strange as it may sound, we are not born to be selfish or to brag about ourselves, but to be servants to others. While this point may be hard to accept, it should be a major part of the purpose of the doctorate degree and the importance of working together to enhance college teaching. Integrity should be a central piece of the doctorate education. Recent graduates should become agents of change with the commitment to the professionalization of exercise physiology, the entrepreneurial spirit, and the willingness to lead.

With the right leadership, exercise physiologists can cultivate discipline with a declaration of intent to speak with optimism and determination to support the long climb of professional development. Yet, on the other hand (which is so common) without authentic leadership, there is no authority and/or integrity. This shows up in several popular exercise physiology textbooks where the authors did not acknowledge exercise physiologists as healthcare professionals.

Fortunately, for 20 years, ASEP has stood the test of time. The leadership has made huge sacrifices in sharing and supporting the need for a vision to align our values, thoughts, and actions to promote the professional growth of exercise physiology. Real faith in who we are is sharing with others that exercise physiology is a healthcare profession, regardless of the colleagues who say otherwise. The possibilities of prescribing exercise to prevent, manage, and treat non-communicable diseases and underlying risk factors are huge for the exercise physiology profession.

With the founding of ASEP, the leadership understood that it was pastime to develop and publish exercise physiology professional issues, organizational concerns, and ethical trends (3). They have made many sacrifices on behalf of all exercise physiologists. Exercise physiology belongs to every college graduate with a degree in exercise physiology whether it is an undergraduate degree or a doctorate degree. In addition, the title, Board Certified Exercise Physiologist, belongs to every person who meets the ASEP requirements to sit and pass the EPC exam.

While you may find these comments strange, please appreciate that several exercise physiologists with the doctorate degree said to me that you cannot allow your students at CSS with an undergraduate degree call themselves an exercise physiologist. It is so disappointing to experience adults living in the past. Can you imagine educated adults making such a comment? Clearly, our colleagues can be educated but also locked in status quo. The first time it happened to me I thought it was 100% a joke. The second time and thereafter caused me to speak out and openly disagree. But, regardless of what I said, my comments were dismissed.

> Successful exercise physiologists look beyond their own personal interests to discover new possibilities.

Individuals who cannot see possibilities refuse to change. No doubt part of the reason is because they are so indoctrinated to think and act as their doctorate professors had said years earlier that thinking different was virtually impossible for them. Thus, regardless of their years of college, it is clear to me that they are unaware of their lack of ability to think straight. Status quo is powerful. It keeps our colleagues from changing and shaping their lives, often in ways that help others to make a difference (4).

Just as exercise is a potent medicine that will help individuals with chronic diseases, learning to consider possibilities as viable options will strengthen the professionalization of exercise physiology. Otherwise, the failure to address this point is strikingly obvious among college teachers who are exercise physiologists. Administrators and faculty members should curb the practice and the relentless pressure to think as they have always done. It is clear that the education of the students is suffering. Why not do the right thing for the right reason?

Also, it is disturbing that since the founding of the *Professionalization of Exercise Physiology-online* (PEPonline) journal in 1998 (5) and the *Journal of Professional Exercise Physiology* (JPEP) in 2003 (6), exercise physiologists at all levels have been slow to publish articles about the importance of professionalism, code of ethics, certification, practice standards, and accreditation. Either the lack of courage to think differently or simply being too busy doing research illustrates the challenge before the ASEP organization to grow exercise physiology.

Exercise Medicine

Yes, the correct term is "exercise medicine"—not exercise is medicine. This is true by the simple example that "physical therapy" is not physical is therapy and "sports medicine" is not sports is medicine. It is a scientific fact that exercise medicine can prevent and treat chronic diseases and disabilities. In fact, since physical inactivity is the major reason for society's high incidence of chronic diseases, it is clear that everyone should get involved in regular exercise as a positive step in taking care of their physical and mental health and well-being.

However, the specifics that undergird exercise medicine are more than just telling an obese teenager or an adult with type 2 diabetes mellitus to go to the gym and exercise. Medicine in the form of exercise requires a prescription just as the medicine Tenormin (atenolol tablets) requires a prescription. It is obvious that a medical doctor prescribes the drug atenolol for hypertension, but it is not so obvious that the healthcare professional who prescribes exercise medicine is a Board Certified Exercise Physiologist (7).

However, from the ASEP perspective, it is reasonable that Board Certified Exercise Physiologist will be recognized as a credible healthcare provider. The reason for this belief is because exercise medicine is not a random exercise intensity prescribed by just anyone with an interest in physical fitness (such as a personal trainer). Therefore, for a medicine to be safe and effective, it must be designed and prescribed by a recognized healthcare professional. Also, that is why the exercise treatment is exercise medicine.

> It seems more than "the right thing to do" that exercise physiologists would demonstrate a continued commitment to professional excellence, scholarship and advancement of exercise physiology.

It is a prescription obtained from an exercise physiologist who is Board Certified. That means the exercise physiologist sat for the ASEP Exercise Physiologist Certified (EPC) exam and passed it. The requirements to sit for the exam are listed on the ASEP website (8). It is a 200 multiple choice exam of which the candidate must score at least 70% to pass. The questions cover such topics as cardiorespiratory physiology, metabolism and muscle contraction, neural muscle function, biomechanics, sports nutrition, electrocardiography, exercise testing and prescription, cardiac rehabilitation, and chronic diseases (9).

The subject matter is engaging and at times very complex. Not just anyone with an undergraduate degree in exercise physiology or a related degree program who meets the criteria to sit for the exam can pass it. That is why ASEP developed the first-ever academic accreditation guidelines for the degree in exercise physiology, the first-ever profession-specific exercise physiology title, and the first-ever exercise physiology-specific curriculum (10).

For certain, just any personal trainer, fitness instructor, or graduate of an exercise science or kinesiology department (regardless of good intentions and experience) cannot pass the exam. The take home message is that many trainers and instructors at Bob's Gym do not have a degree in exercise physiology or (in many cases) even a related academic degree to qualify them to prescribe exercise medicine. They are not academically prepared to evaluate, test, and supervise the prescriptive aspects of exercise medicine unique to clients and/or patients with chronic diseases and/or disabilities.

> The issue of professional development must be dissected, shared, and applied by all exercise physiologists.

This thinking is not complicated. It is the truth, and it is no different from the academic and professional expectations of other healthcare professionals. But, and this is the point of this chapter, the academic exercise physiologists are not open to possibilities as they should be (particularly the role of ASEP in healthcare). Either they do not acknowledge exercise physiology as a healthcare profession or they are simply too buried in their own self-interests of publishing research papers to give time to the profession of exercise physiology (11).

The failure to look ahead is not helping the students of exercise physiology. Moreover, it is very much like driving in the dark without lights or the knowledge of why lights are even required to prevent an accident. Therefore, to do so is to work against logical and rational thinking and that is exactly what exercise physiologists at all academic levels are doing when they turn a deaf ear to supporting the ASEP organization and vision (12).

Final Thoughts

When exercise physiologists fail to be open to new ideas, to changing, and to possibility thinking, it is almost impossible to avoid doing the wrong thing. Yet, there is no reason why exercise physiologists must be failures. So, why not stand up and become proactive in the pursuit of excellence, which begins with the ASEP work with the promotion of professionalism in exercise physiology (13). The leadership is eager to learn of other exercise physiologists with the drive to knock on the ASEP door to share in cleaning up the mess of decades of lack of discipline and tenacity for healthcare possibilities.

> Organizations, like ASEP, that maintain their core values stand for something.

Exercise physiologists must show some backbone if they are to commit to change. The indifference to ASEP professional effort and credentials in the practice of exercise physiology is wrong (14). By parallel, imagine where athletic trainers would be had they failed to change from where they were decades ago. The short answer is they would not exist as they presently do. Society would not recognize them as important to athletics and sports and yet, they took the risk of being themselves and it paid off. That takes courage and guts.

Other professions have demonstrated the same desire and accountability. They have been willing to face the challenges and learn from their mistakes. Exercise physiologists must make the commitment to do the same. It is time to cut the generic organizational umbilical cord. It is time to encourage curiosity, to take a chance, to persevere, and to stop being governed by illusion and deception. After all, "Persistence and determination alone are omnipotent" (15).

References

1 Boone, T. (2001). *Professional Development of Exercise Physiology*. Lewiston, NY: The Edwin Mellen Press.
2 Boone, T. (2005). *Exercise Physiology: Professional Issues, Organizational Concerns, and Ethical Trends*. Lewiston, NY: The Edwin Mellen Press.
3 Boone, T. (2006). *Exercise Physiology as a Career: A Guide and Sourcebook*. Lewiston, NY: The Edwin Mellen Press.
4 Schuller, R. A. (1987). *Power to Grow Beyond Yourself*. Old Tappan, NJ: Fleming H. Revell Company.
5 American Society of Exercise Physiologists. (2017). Professionalization of Exercise Physiology-online. (Online). www.asep.org/index.php/resources/pep-online/.
6 American Society of Exercise Physiologists. (2017). Journal of Professional Exercise Physiology. (Online). www.asep.org/index.php/resources/journal-professional-exercise-physiology/.
7 Boone, T. (2007). *Ethical Standards and Professional Credentials in the Practice of Exercise Physiology*. Lewiston, NY: The Edwin Mellen Press.
8 Boone, T. (2009). *The Professionalization of Exercise Physiology: Certification, Accreditation, and Standards of Practice of the American Society of Exercise Physiologists (ASEP)*. Lewiston, NY: The Edwin Mellen Press.
9 Boone, T. (2013). *Introduction to Exercise Physiology*. Burlington, MA: Jones & Bartlett Learning.
10 Boone, T. (2015). *Professionalism in Exercise Physiology*. Lewiston, NY: The Edwin Mellen Press.
11 Boone, T. (2016). *ASEP's Exercise Medicine Text for Exercise Physiologists*. Beijing, China: Bentham Science Publishers.
12 American Society of Exercise Physiologists. (2017). ASEP Vision. (Online). www.asep.org/index.php/about-asep/.
13 American Society of Exercise Physiologists. (2017). The ASEP Vision Statement. (Online). www.asep.org/index.php/organization/.
14 American Society of Exercise Physiologists. (2017). Standards of Practice. (Online). www.asep.org/index.php/organization/practice/.
15 Kroc, R. A. (1978). *Grinding It Out*. New York: Berkley Books, p. 201.

3
STUDENTS OR RESEARCH

For more than four decades I shared classrooms, offices, and laboratories with exercise physiologists in six academic institutions. Singly and collectively, we published research, presented research papers at national and regional meetings, introduced students to metabolic analyzers, treadmills protocols, and cycle ergometer tests, and of course we taught the common list of courses during the fall, spring, and summer semesters. Most of the time, these responsibilities were performed without reflection, as is true with many academic exercise physiologists today. And yet, it is important to point out that the increased emphasis on research created tension with the faculty members who were more interested in teaching than in doing research.

> College teachers must realize that teaching is their priority. Chairs, vice-presidents, and other administrators should rethink the illusion that students learn from the departments' research.

I understand the desire to publish. I was once a college professor who was driven to find the right journal for my recently completed manuscript. But, after my first 20 years of college teaching, I realized the emphasis on research empowered me more than it helped my students. While occasionally it was appropriate to use a few of the research articles in my exercise physiology lectures, it was always more important to emphasize the exercise physiology content from a textbook.

Ask yourself this question, "What is the primary responsibility of a college teacher?" Clearly, the administrators, particularly the department chairs, deans, and vice-presidents talk a lot about faculty publishing and securing grants with the expectation of bringing in money for the purchase of expensive equipment. Why?

Sean Carroll (1) hit the nail on the head when he said, "... because money is good, and it's extremely quantifiable." The faculty also uses publishing to elevate the institution in the eyes of the public. In fact, if a faculty member is exceptional at publishing, it is essentially a home run for tenure and a reduced teaching load.

Also, it is important to understand what Peter S. Cahn (2) said regarding the public research university.

> I felt immediately comfortable in the anthropology department. This was the type of campus where I had studied, and the expectations for junior faculty members were transparent. "To get tenure," the department chairwoman told me at our first meeting, "you need a book or a series of articles. If you have great publications but lousy teaching, you'll still get tenure. If you have great teaching but not-so-great publications, you won't get tenure." Her bluntness confirmed what I had always suspected and reassured me of the university's priorities.

Sean Carroll (1) also said, "... the purpose of Harvard is not to educate students. If anything, its primary purpose is to produce research and scholarly work." The endowment of $35 billion in 2008 was not to produce the best teachers. Instead, it was used to "... build new facilities, launch new research initiatives, and attract the best faculty" (1).

College professors are presently valued for their research. They are not valued for their teaching skills. Their research is considered an excellent investment while the teachers' ability to teach and engage students is of a secondary interest. In agreement, Lucas Carpenter (3) said, "... no university ever became world class by virtue of the quality of its teaching." Obviously, the belief exists that what distinguishes great professors from merely good ones is research. It isn't the professors' cognitive skills, emotional intelligence, or big-picture thinking.

I have found, however, that the most effective college professors are alike in one crucial way: They all have a profound interest in building the students' strengths, helping them understand the importance of persistence and practice, and to "know thyself." One thing is certain: Efforts should be made to promote excellence in teaching. To enhance the students' educational experience, college professors must refocus their thinking to include a greater emphasis on teaching.

Although the exercise physiology professors in the exercise science and kinesiology departments have not come together as an exercise physiology profession, they should for numerous reasons. If they were to, it would mean they understand the need to think out of the box from the decades of personalized opinions as to what is kinesiology, for example, and how is it different from exercise science or human performance (4)? And yet, the faculty in each of these areas seems to think it is better to remain unchanged than to evolve into a unified profession of exercise physiologists. As a result of the fragmentation in their thinking and the resulting lack of a vision of something better for themselves and their students, the payoff in better-paying job opportunities and a more fulfilling life after college doesn't exist.

Consider the case of the college graduate who is better off with a high income versus a low income or no income. This is the desired path, and for good reason. There is the opportunity to buy a house, a car, and meet monthly financial obligations when hired into a career-specific income. The established professions seem to know intuitively that this approach makes sense. Also, given that this thinking is the students' reality for going to college, then getting a college degree is better understood when they hand over their parents' hard-earned money or their own borrowed money to colleges throughout the United States to pay tuition fees and living expenses.

A Career Driven Degree

While exercise science professors have yet to understand the importance of a career driven academic degree, the thought itself is pleasure to the ears of students who have taken the time to think about what it means to be responsible for their financial existence. Their thinking goes something like this: "I can be successful. I will be successful. My parents will be proud of me. I am majoring in a career driven degree. I understand that not all degrees are created equal." Why college professors are not interested in the reasons high school graduates go to college is strange and wrong. They need to be more transparent as to value of the exercise science degree after college, especially when the faculty members are constantly planning for their own success.

> Unless you are an excellent entrepreneur, you need a college degree to get a job and pay check to pay back the college tuition loan, rent for housing, monthly car note, as well as the purchase of food and other necessities of life. But, of course, the barrier to living the dream of a better life is dependent upon the quality of the academic degree.

While chairpersons, faculty, and deans may argue that college graduates are prepared for a career in the public sector that will lay the foundation for their success, they are wrong when it comes to the academic degree programs that are offshoots of physical education of the 1960s. We all know that degree programs such as kinesiology, exercise science, human performance, and sports science are meaningless when it comes to producing a financially sustainable career (4).

As we all know, academic exercise physiologists are either not aware of this problem or they simply refuse to think about it. After all, they have a pretty good paying job, health insurance, and other benefits. It is clear that the professors will do essentially anything to keep it their job. The shame of the higher education is that the benefits are specific to the tenured faculty who represent 17% of college instructors (5).

The concern of the 21st century should be to what extent are the academic institutions properly serving students. Specifically, the question is this: "Is it ethical a college degree is not linked to a career that increases employment prospects and earnings?" The answer is "No." In particular, can the exercise science degree actually help the majority of the students after graduation to attain a better quality of life? Again, the answer is "Not."

Answers to these questions are critical to the purpose of a college education and why students are paying such high tuition dollars with a huge loan debt. Also important is the concern that the exercise physiology students are not being taught how to think as healthcare professionals, how to develop individualized exercise medicine prescriptions, and how to start an entrepreneurial business.

To make matters worse, the exercise physiology faculty fails in providing students information that is accurate about the exercise physiology degree. For example, is the degree valued by physicians? Do nurses and other healthcare professionals understand the role of the exercise physiologist in healthcare? This is a concern that needs immediate attention, especially since misinformation can't help the students. That said, the failure to update degree programs with career-specific opportunities also impact the students' parents and family members. It is one thing to finish college with a high debt and find a job, and something else altogether different for students to graduate with thousands of dollars in debt and find themselves living at home with their parents.

Understandably, these concerns are not unique to the for-profit institutions since it is common knowledge that academic non-profit institutions are out to make a profit as well. When it comes to the exercise science and related degree programs, the majority of the state colleges and universities are just as bad. Apparently, they lack the desire and/or will to address the importance of changing the academic degree title to exercise physiology, the necessity of revising the curriculum and becoming an ASEP accredited institution, owning up to the ethical standards of practice, and professionalism (6).

As a result, there are dozens of degree programs without a recognized professional credential and without career-specific jobs. The faculty, chairs, deans, and vice-presidents are not thinking about the specific needs of their students. Therefore, without real job opportunities, the degree programs are a waste of time and money. Just because the faculty realized decades ago that their job is secure as long as they publish an article or two every year in a high impact journal does not mean they can simply avoid the ethical responsibility of changing how they think. It is also wrong to do nothing to improve the students' education while advising them to apply to graduate school or to physical therapy. While it is the faculty's formula for continued success, students graduate without a job, in debt, disappointed, and depressed (7).

Strangely enough, the majority of the college teachers in exercise science (many who refer to themselves as exercise scientists and exercise physiologists) go from one semester to the next, year after year without asking the following questions:

1. Is the exercise science degree a good financial investment?
2. Would I encourage my son or daughter to major in exercise science?
3. Will the exercise science degree help students move beyond their personal training job at Bob's Gym?
4. Will the exercise science degree provide the majority of the college graduates a credible job with the financial income to pay their student loans and still afford a mortgage?
5. Does the exercise science degree benefit society or does it exist as a feeder program for existing healthcare professions?
6. Does the exercise science degree exist in the department to benefit the faculty more than the students?
7. Given that the college tuition per year has skyrocketed and graduates find themselves either unemployed or stuck in jobs that do not require a bachelor's degree, should the chair of the department (and/or exercise science faculty) request a meeting to discuss changes in the program?
8. Why is it that the academic exercise physiologists, who understand the significance of exercise medicine, are not updating the exercise science degree to exercise physiology with an entrepreneurial thinking strategy so that the college graduates will know how to create their own Exercise Medicine Clinic?

Aside from the faculty of kinesiology, exercise science, and exercise physiology lacking the desire to upgrade to an ASEP exercise physiology degree title and curriculum, they have spent little to no time during the past 20 years addressing the importance of a degree-driven career. Unfortunately, this is in addition to the fact that the students are not asking questions about job employment opportunities after college (as they should). In fact, many students come across as not being interested in a credible academic major. One reason is their first love is sports. It is true that many students are comfortable with the teachers' lack of a strong emphasis on teaching, and the teachers (as expected) are comfortable with their pursuit of academic advancement and tenure.

> The bad news is that the majority of the undergraduates do not realize that the majority of the academic degrees are not designed to help students find a credible job after college.

While the full-time teachers are responsible for research, teaching, and service, there should be more emphasis placed on teaching than is presently the case. It is unacceptable that Ph.D. programs do not take the time to provide doctorate students with a course or training in how to teach. Not surprisingly, the question is this: "Why isn't there a better doctorate education?" All adjunct and full-time professors should have pedagogical training to develop their teaching skills.

While faculty publications in books, journals, and conferences are essential to academic advancement, department chairs should be concerned about high-quality learning, evidence-based inquiry and reasoning, and far-reaching entrepreneur innovations. Students at all levels need the help of the faculty and administrators interested in helping them achieve their career goals. Going the extra mile is the work that still needs to be done to help students and their parents understand the importance of majoring in a high-quality undergraduate degree program.

Exercise Physiology in Higher Education

Higher education is special or at least it should be. After all, what is after high school ... work or college or both? The fact is that the majority of the students do both for four or more years to earn a college degree. Higher education is the primary method by which young men and women gain access to professionally credible and financially sound career opportunities. Of course, there is also the expectation of the never-ending search for truth in knowledge. It is of utmost important that the recently graduated student transitions from college to the public sector with the knowledge, attitude, and skills to help others and him- or herself.

It is the ethical responsibility of college teachers to higher education to avoid pontification and saying that this degree is simply a transitional step to some other academic program (such as physical therapy or nursing). In fact, it is in their best interest to make a full analysis of the factors that contribute to the students' success and failure after graduation. The faculty members who achieve tenure should understand this thinking and yet, strangely enough the reality of higher education suggests otherwise.

> More exercise physiologists are waking up to their higher potential and recognizing that there are credible healthcare career opportunities that are accessible to all Board Certified Exercise Physiologists.

I am aware that life is complicated and higher education is important for obvious reasons but coming to understand the narrow and often isolated thinking of most faculty members is disappointing. Why they have stopped learning remains a disappointment that should be analyzed and understood? The public should know what their reasons are for neglecting professionalism. Is it as simple as spending more time on research projects? Growth in excellence as a teacher and as an exercise physiologist is dependent on the professors' understanding of the importance of professionalism as well as the mind and body factors that influence health and well-being (8).

Beneath all this there is a deeper paradox. Although it is true that exercise physiologists are constantly doing research, they differ from other doctorate prepared healthcare professionals in that they fail to understand the overwhelming importance of belonging to and supporting their own profession and professional organization. Such overt failure and lack of empathy represent a generation of failed thinking that is destroying the academic atmosphere of good will and mutual trust.

The ASEP exercise physiologists have moved beyond the age-old idea that a college teacher is just a researcher. They understand the importance of a well-designed educational program that increases the students understanding of the content that undergirds exercise physiology. But to fulfill the role of being a teacher beyond superficial qualities that can be very deceptive, there must be the desire to find the truth beyond status quo (9). So, why not acknowledge the present-day mistakes and start learning from them and keep going toward our goals of empowering the students and embracing exercise physiology as a healthcare profession?

Future education will require college professors to teach the importance of professionalism and the meaning of credibility as a healthcare professional. Their students will learn the complexity of these topics and how to emerge with influence on other exercise physiologists. The professors will unravel the mystery of changing how they think to make it possible to take the first step to develop a course to teach professional development. Such a course will involve analyzing "where we are" and "where we are going" as a profession in healthcare. It will also involve weighing the relative merits of that which are written, spoken, or thought on behalf of all students who want to be an exercise physiologist.

Thus, the responsible and honest college teachers will find the time and opportunity to pursue the truth. They will learn the value in distinguishing the significant path from the trivial, especially when the latter is driven by non-exercise physiologists of generic organizations. They will learn to ask insightful, meaningful, and direct questions about the origin of exercise physiology and its relationship to a career in healthcare. Fortunately, the straight-thinking exercise physiologists understand this point, and they are not dragging their feet. They are ready to share the ASEP truths with their students.

The students will learn that their teachers are not supporting status quo merely for the sake of disagreement, nor do they make arguments just to do so. There is a purpose in the examination of what is versus what should be. They understand the value in distinguishing between the relevant and the irrelevant thinking that provides continuity and support for the change process. This is especially evident when it is apparent mediocrity is a mental condition that drives the lack of independence of mind and the subjugation of relevant and proven ideas.

The desire to change and support professional development does not come naturally. The seed of its necessity compared to the alternative drives the process, especially when nourished by the reality and courage of colleagues (e.g., the conviction of physical therapists speaks volumes). The PTs independence and dedication to professionalism in physical therapy promote and sustain students and the profession, which causes a person to believe in the process.

First, it is important to understand the influence of non-exercise physiologists as a negative force to be dealt with. A second requisite is the opportunity to pursue the belief that professionalism in exercise physiology is worth developing, and that it will be sustained by the ASEP vision. This means there must be the opportunity to think differently from yesterday's way of thinking. Uncommon ideas must be allowed, given that they will set the stage for personal reflection, speculation, and analysis of present day dogma.

> ASEP has forced some exercise physiologists to reconsider "what is", where they have examined their values, questioned their assumptions about generic organizations, and helped others to share their values and thinking.

Third, students will grasp the expectation and right to major in an exercise physiology degree by title, not an exercise physiology look alike degree. They have the right to expect that their professors will play a large role in cultivating and nourishing the existence of and the potentially new career opportunities to help ensure their success after college. Similarly, it is the students' prerogative to expect that their educational journey will be enriched by faculty guidance driven by the spirit and necessity of professionalism.

Fourth, the teaching–learning relationship will support the shared thinking of professionalism across the healthcare professions. This means that academic exercise physiologists will learn to show an active interest in talking about the ASEP code of ethics, accreditation guidelines, board certification, and standards of practice (6). The faculty will demonstrate concern for their students' problems by promoting and publishing professionalism research, articles, and books. To deny this direction of purposeful expectation and work is to negate the value of what the established professions have already done.

Fifth, as daunting as it may seem, essential to the transformative mindset is the necessity to learn, practice, and implement the merits of professional development. Building a shared vision of exercise physiology as a healthcare profession is critical to sustaining the ASEP vision and mindset that exercise physiologists are more than just their research papers. They are healthcare professionals with the desire and ability to share their reality with the world. Hence, however uncomfortable or mentally difficult it is to change, the desire and willingness to do so will sustain the commitment.

Final Thoughts

A great injustice lies in failing to know specifically "what is exercise physiology" and "who is an exercise physiologist" and why both are essential to promote and develop professionalism in exercise physiology. Exercise physiologists with and without the doctorate degree must come together in the freedom of thought and action to create an image of what they want to be. The temptation to conform to yesterday's thinking must be replaced by an updated intellectual curiosity, an aptitude, and a strong personal willingness for professional development, and the desire and power to leverage new ideas and concepts.

This necessity to choose a different path is fundamental to the concept of academic freedom. For this reason, each academic and non-academic exercise physiologist must explore what he or she is, why he or she is doing it, and doing whatever is believed to be the next step that is necessary to assume responsibility for what is right and what is wrong with the way and manner exercise physiologists define and perform as exercise medicine professionals. The need for identifying their true purpose and direction in higher education in the midst of stupidity and lack of faith by many colleagues is great.

Young professors cannot allow their sense of work to be defined by just publishing research articles. Research is important but so are the responsibilities of teaching and professionalism. College teachers are responsible for educating students without distorting the truth of the problems that stem from indoctrination and indifference. While playing the conformity game is thought to be prerequisite to success, in reality it is the ultimate failure in personal autonomy, freedom, and independence. Instead, we must develop our own sense of identity just as other prominent healthcare professionals have done. The commitment to our students is a strong beginning, but exercise physiologists must also be committed to each other.

When you picture an academic institution with its faculty and curricula, what one word comes to mind? It is "service." The institution's purpose is to serve students. They do not exist to serve the faculty's interest, regardless of the faculty's expectation otherwise. When the latter is the case, the students' education suffers as well as their career opportunities and personal success after college. The faculty-centered academic environment versus the student-centered environment needs changing. The faculty must be willing to see the difference between "what is" and "what should be."

Trust is a powerful means of dealing with the fear of change, the fear of being ridiculed, and the uncomfortable feelings of being different. This is why building personal relationships and one-to-one opportunities to visit, talk, and share ideas and possibilities are important during the change process. Collectively, they help to secure one's voice in promoting new teaching strategies and innovative plans to help students think about and visualize their future as exercise physiologists. This shift in perception from being researchers to teachers will be acknowledged as a positive mental, social, and professional step for all exercise physiologists.

References

1 Carroll, S. (2011). How to Get Tenure at a Major Research University (Online). *Discover*. http://blogs.discovermagazine.com/cosmicvariance/2011/03/30/how-to-get-tenure-at-a-major-research-university/#.WKI7Y9IrJ0w.
2 Cahn, P. (2002). Teaching versus Research (Online). *The Chronicle of Higher Education*. www.chronicle.com/article/Teaching-Versus-Research/45969.
3 Carpenter, L. (2003). Teaching versus Research: Does It Have to Be That Way? (Online). *The Academic Exchange*. www.emory.edu/ACAD_EXCHANGE/2003/sept/carpenter.html.
4 Boone, T. (2001). *Professional Development of Exercise Physiology*. Lewiston, NY: The Edwin Mellen Press.

5 Birmingham, K. (2017). The Great Shame of Our Profession (Online). *The Chronicle of Higher Education*. www.chronicle.com/article/The-Great-Shame-of-Our/239148.
6 Boone, T. (2009). *The Professionalization of Exercise Physiology: Certification, Accreditation, and Standards of Practice of the American Society of Exercise Physiologists (ASEP)*. Lewiston, NY: The Edwin Mellen Press.
7 Boone, T. (2005). *Exercise Physiology: Professional Issues, Organizational Concerns, and Ethical Trends*. Lewiston, NY: The Edwin Mellen Press.
8 Boone, T. (2016). *ASEP's Exercise Medicine Text for Exercise Physiologists*. Beijing, China: Bentham Science Publishing.
9 Boone, T. (2014). Problems and Opportunities in Exercise Physiology Higher Education. *Journal of Professional Physiology*. 12;10:1–4.

4
NEW LEADERSHIP

Recently, I received an email from a person who asked the question: "Is ASEP a leader in exercise physiology?" While leadership is defined in many different ways, I could not help but say, "Yes, of course!" In 1997, the ASEP leaders understood the importance of a vision. They had a dream, and they still believe in the dream. They believe ASEP will help: (a) produce new career opportunities for the students of exercise physiology; (b) unify exercise physiologists as exercise medicine professionals; (c) support the vision, standards of professional practice, and professionalization of exercise physiologists; and (d) empower the members to serve the public good by making an academically sound difference in the application of exercise physiology concepts and insights.

More than Just Research

Creating and expressing a vision is an important part of leading others. ASEP is all about exercise physiology as a healthcare profession. ASEP Board Certified exercise physiologists are the experts in prescribing exercise medicine. The leadership believes that exercise physiology is more than the academic exercise physiologists publishing research papers and undergraduate students becoming personal trainers and fitness instructors.

The ASEP leaders believe the academic major in exercise physiology should be about graduating students as professionals in healthcare. And, just for the record, ASEP does not have an issue with the good that technicians, instructors, and trainers do in society. But, the simple fact is this: A fitness instructor or a personal trainer is not an academically prepared exercise physiologist who administers exercise medicine as treatment for chronic diseases and disabilities.

While some trainers are good at leading fitness programs, the ASEP's point of view is entirely different thinking from what is heard in generic organizations such as ACSM. What is needed today are exercise physiologists with the courage to acknowledge why a "college education" is supposed to be "a credible career credential" and not a degree to apply to graduate school.

Yet, the latter is exactly the case today and it is wrong. Cautious academics are doing their best to keep exercise physiology in the 20th century. A better world means it is better for everyone and not just for the doctorate prepared exercise physiologists who more often than not find excellent career opportunities in academia. The ASEP leaders realize that a trainer's job at Bob's Gym is not a credible career option to raise a family. They get that Bob's Gym may be a place for college students who are working on a degree, but it isn't the destination point after college.

Thus, the bottom line is this: ASEP has a different view of the importance of an academic degree than the majority of the academic exercise physiologists, especially when it comes to the degree in exercise physiology. The organization supports the belief that the undergraduate degree must have career significance. Students must not be told when they are about the graduate that they must apply to graduate school and get a master's degree or apply to another major altogether!

For years, the ASEP leaders have hear parents asked the question: "Why wasn't my son made aware of this point when he was convinced four years ago by the department faculty that it was a great idea to major in exercise science?"

It is common knowledge that there is a high tuition debt and graduation cost associated with attending college. To help offset the debt and cost, the college degree is supposed to be about turning hopes and dreams into the reality of being financially successful after college. Yet, the truth is many degree programs are an illusion, and students are at considerable risk of huge debt after college with no way to pay for it. That is why the ASEP organization cannot support the exercise science mentality that is shared with thousands of students throughout the United States. Clearly, the idea itself is unethical behavior because the academic exercise physiologists and other supporting faculty members already know there are few credible jobs with a major in exercise science.

The ASEP leaders believe the lack of jobs can be reversed with the right thinking and desire to work on behalf of the students. They believe the exercise science degree should be updated to exercise physiology, and an entirely new way of thinking about exercise should be that exercise physiologists are leader in exercise medicine. This means that such thinking must be acknowledged by the chairperson and the faculty of the department who are responsible for providing an ethically sound academic major. Also, they must want to help in the professional development of exercise physiologists as well as the ASEP Board Certification that is prerequisite to practicing as an ASEP Board Certified Exercise Physiologist with the expectation to prescribe exercise medicine.

In short, it is the responsibility of the faculty to do everything necessary to create a better future for all the students of exercise physiology. They should have the ability to imagine themselves in their students' shoes and to feel with their hearts. Empathy allows the faculty to "feel the students' pain". After all, leadership should be about relating and connecting with students for the purpose of helping them, perhaps, as healthcare entrepreneurs to promote professionalism in exercise physiology (1).

But, the question is: Where is the leadership in exercise physiology? Robert Greenleaf said it better, "We should be servant leaders, those who first serve others and whose primary motivation is a desire to help others" (2). Exercise physiology needs leadership that offers hope and guidance for a new era in exercise physiology development, for the creation of a better academic degree, and for more caring of the students of academic institutions.

> **DARE TO BE DIFFERENT**
>
> So, let me get this right. You are afraid of being different. That is why you dress the way you do, and why you will not join ASEP. Wow, I thought you understood it was necessary to challenge the exercise science status quo to grow exercise physiology. Why not observe what your colleagues are doing, and try to do the opposite and see what happens?

The ASEP leaders believe exercise physiologists should dare to be different. But, strangely enough, thinking as a healthcare professional is out of the question for most academics. They fail to grasp the meaning of the revolution that drives the Board Certified Exercise Physiologists who see themselves as the next generation of servant leaders in healthcare.

Although the work of ASEP is a relatively silent revolution, it is alive and well. Driven by compassion and respect, the noble intentions of the ASEP organization are to produce changes in how exercise physiologists think of each other. There is also the intent to build on values that will serve to help academic exercise physiologists to think of themselves differently. This is important since they see themselves as researchers who avoid criticism at all costs, which is problematic for several reasons. In particular, their lifestyle is consistent with the thinking of Aristotle who said: "Criticism is something you can easily avoid by saying nothing, doing nothing, and being nothing" (3).

The ASEP exercise physiologists care about the future of college students. That is why they are willing to accept criticism on behalf of improving exercise physiology. Criticism will not stop them from dreaming about a better future for all students of exercise physiology. They want to help others be successful rather than to be more successful themselves. They believe today's students need face-to-face academic and professional leadership to change the fixed mindset of many for the better. That is why they are retooling and seeking resolution of shared issues by promoting discussion about leadership, professional development, exercise physiology professionalism, ethical thinking as exercise physiologists, healthcare reform, and career decision-making.

Exercise physiology is moving from the "acute and chronic adaptations to exercise and sports" mentality to exercise medicine with a healthcare emphasis. Exercise physiologists of the future will pay less attention to sports and athletics and more attention to the prescription of exercise medicine in the treatment of chronic diseases and disabilities in all age groups and gender. Board Certified Exercise Physiologists will not only determine a client and/or patient's cardiac, respiratory, and metabolic responses to an exercise test, but will use regression equations to provide physiologic feedback (4) to highlight the power of the mind in preventing diseases, as well as the role of spirituality in health and well-being (5).

> ASEP exercise physiologists are avoiding mediocrity by daring to be different. They get that life is too important to live an average or ordinary life.

This way of thinking is a dream and a vision. The truth is life is too precious to be lived in mediocrity. Fortunately, the ASEP Board Certified Exercise Physiologists have an extensive scientific knowledge base supported by critical thinking skills and sophisticated hands-on laboratory skills that will help them to become an essential reality within the healthcare practice. All that is needed now are more exercise physiologists who are willing to assert themselves and to think positive when working to overcome status quo and the dogma of academic institutions and the mindset of generic organizations.

The fact that student loans outstanding in 2010, both federal and private, consisted of some $829.785 billion means something has to change. The fact that the nation's collective student loan debt exceeded its collective credit card debt for the first time in history means there is a problem and it needs fixing. Students and their parents from all across the United States should not be placed in the financial chaos and emotional pain that academic institutions create.

The ASEP faculty members are passionate about making a difference in society's views and expectations of exercise physiologists, particularly in the delivery of clinical exercise prescriptions for the prevention or management of chronic and complex healthcare conditions. They realize that exercise physiologists are key players in shaping the future of exercise physiology as a healthcare profession, not just as a discipline or whatever else is being considered by the non-exercise physiologists. They realize that in some cases, aside from improving the immune system and helping to delay cognitive impairment, regular exercise is better than traditional prescription drugs when it comes to preventing chronic conditions such as coronary heart disease, stroke, and diabetes.

A contemporary piece of advice from Sheila C. Grossman and Theresa M. Valiga, authors of the book, *The New Leadership Challenge: Creating the Future of Nursing* (6), captures the essence of leadership and involvement in exercise physiology as it does in nursing:

Excellence can be attained if you ...
  CARE more than others think is wise,
  RISK more than others think is safe,
  DREAM more than others think is practical, and
  EXPECT more than others think is possible.

Commitment to Professionalism

Ask yourself the following questions. Do you think recent graduates with a major in exercise physiology look forward to the day when society recognizes them as healthcare professionals and not as trainers, given the association with exercise science? Do you think a new academic exercise physiologist who has been given responsibility to teach exercise science in the Department of Kinesiology will ask him or herself the question: "Why haven't the chairperson and the faculty worked together to rename the department and the academic degree to exercise physiology?"

> If exercise physiologists are seeking to be recognized in healthcare, they must tell themselves that they have faith in their practice of exercise physiology, and in the certainty of exercise medicine to promote health and well-being.

As a college teacher I can tell you that almost every conversation I had with a faculty member from biology, business, nursing, or chemistry, I was asked the question: "What sport do you coach?" Almost without thinking I would say, "No, I am not a coach. I am an exercise physiologist." Then, I would be asked the question: "What do you teach?" I would say: "Each semester I teach a combination of courses, such as cardiorespiratory physiology, gross anatomy (with cadaver dissection), exercise metabolism, psychophysiology of health and fitness, graded exercise testing, and electrocardiography." The response was almost always, "What?" The problem is that even our academic colleagues from other departments know little about what academic exercise physiologists do and, yet everyone understands what the nurse, physical therapist, and athletic trainer does.

For decades academic exercise physiologists have failed to educate the upper academic administration and the public sector as to their scientific training and healthcare expertise, which has no doubt limited career opportunities for college graduates. Fortunately, with the help of the ASEP members and the gradual changes within the academic infrastructure, it is becoming increasingly clear that exercise physiologists are healthcare professionals. That is why it is necessary that the ASEP seed of freedom is planted throughout academia and society.

But first, academic exercise physiologists must be responsible for promoting professionalism in exercise physiology. This means that exercise physiologists should not say, "I am too busy doing research to think about our own professional organization." Change is all about the collective effort of every faculty member who is an exercise physiologist. The power to achieve change in how others view exercise physiology exists primarily with the faculty, the department chairs, and the administration. Remember, it is better to give than to receive if the students are to experience new career opportunities and new professional possibilities.

The science of change means that exercise physiologists must learn to take responsibility for their own future. Along the way, exercise physiologists will find a better place for their work and a higher standard for all students of exercise physiology. Hence, if exercise physiologists are truly worthy of society's attention, then, as long as they believe they are worthy, their thinking will create real value in society. This is also why we must immerse ourselves in positive thinking and new possibilities for the students of exercise physiology. Our belief is everything and more! So, never stop believing and never quit doing your best.

Exercise physiologists with the right attitudes are likely to not stop thinking of themselves as healthcare professionals. The more they can consciously take responsibility for the acknowledgment of exercise physiologists as healthcare professionals, the more completely they will believe it and the more powerful they will become in helping society grow stronger and more durable with less disease and disability. Admittedly, it takes discipline and courage and, yes, it takes faith too (7).

The realization exercise physiologists have the right education to prescribe exercise medicine is supported by research, an ASEP accredited exercise physiology curriculum, and hands-on laboratory skills. Thus, once the academic exercise physiologist links research with healthcare and exercise physiology as a profession, the expectation of increased career opportunities will be the students' reward. But, they must discover what to believe in, why they believe in it, and have the faith and peace of mind to act on it no matter what happens.

Exercise physiologists must move away from the conventional wisdom of the sports medicine and exercise science if they are going to be successful solving the unique challenges they face. Our reality comes from within us. So, if you are an academic exercise physiologist, it is should not be necessary to explain to a colleague what you do at work. It should be enough to say: "As an exercise physiologist, I am a member of the ASEP profession of healthcare practitioners who support their own profession-specific organization. Singly and collectively, we prescribe exercise medicine to prevent and/or treat chronic diseases and disabilities." The specifics of this kind of thinking are vitally important in that it is almost certain that exercise physiology as a healthcare profession will not survive if it is not part of its own professional organization.

We must become actively constructive and forward thinking to move from a research discipline to a healthcare profession.

The fundamental premise upon which professionalism is understood, taught, and comprehended by members of a profession is one of higher thoughts and nobler deeds. It is not about money or making more money, however important. Professionalism is built upon the ASEP beliefs about what is exercise physiology, the acceptance that exercise physiologists have a unique scientific understanding of the human body and the laboratory skills that separate them from personal trainers and fitness instructors, and the trust and faith (i.e., conviction) that comes with a strong sense of self-esteem.

Final Thoughts

Because our work today towards professionalism brings forth something that is better than what exercise physiology was yesterday, exercise physiologists are becoming less influenced by the failed promises of non-exercise physiologists and more willing to be led by their own thoughts and ideas. This is the beginning of amazing changes to reshape our professional lives and our profession-specific organization.

Regardless of the challenges and criticisms, the ASEP organization will come out on top. Exercise physiologists will be recognized as healthcare leaders in prescribing exercise medicine. They will enjoy greater career success along with happier work conditions. This means exercise physiologists are resolutely turning away from status quo and from other experiences that have kept exercise physiology from growing.

It is inevitable the day shall come when an understanding and cooperation will be recognized between medical doctors and exercise physiologists. Until that day arrives, exercise physiologists must believe in themselves, their work, and their determination to sustain the transition from being a discipline to a healthcare profession.

> Every evolving profession must pay the price for that which it receives, and that price is paid in work, new experiences, and the will of its members to fully express themselves to realize their destiny (regardless of the criticism).

Change is not an idea that happens overnight. It is a continuous process of new ideas, making the right choices, staying strong, and standing up to obstacles. After all, exercise physiologists have the right to their own future even though it is perceived as impossible by many.

It is your choice to support creating what did not exist before the founding of ASEP. It has always been a decision that is made at your level of consciousness. You can join the ASEP organization and draw closer to its vision than you have ever been before or stay anchored to the past. Your colleagues may want you believe that, "Exercise science is the way we have always done it." Everyone loves status quo. Why, because the past way of thinking is often viewed as safe and comfortable. That is why most people will do almost anything to avoid changing, even if it means engaging in meaningless and unethical behaviors that result in more mediocrity and misguided thinking.

It should be obvious by now making the choice to be different, to think different from others, and to create a dynamic tomorrow with ASEP as the organization for exercise physiologists isn't going to happen in a flash. It takes diligence to change. But, given the new kind of healthcare possibilities and career success, commitment will happen as we recognize our strengths within us and our willingness to invent our own solutions. That is why dreaming the big dreams help. Also, thinking the right thoughts help, especially given the awesome truth, as Robert A. Schuller (7) says, "The person you see is the person you'll be."

What does it mean to be a leader in exercise physiology? It is a matter of putting yourself, your students, and exercise physiology first. Leadership is not about publishing as much as you can to build your own ego or curriculum vitae. Being a good leader isn't about "what's in it for me." It is about standing up against the forces of yesterday's thinking and doing what you can to create what has never before existed.

References

1 Boone, T. (2001). *Professional Development of Exercise. Physiology*. Lewiston, NY: The Edwin Mellen Press.
2 Greenleaf, R. K. (2008). *The Servant as Leader*. Westfield, IN: The Greenleaf Center for Servant Leadership.
3 Aristotle's Quote (Online). *ThinkExist.com*. http://thinkexist.com/quotation/criticism_is_something_we_can_avoid_easily_by/178268.html.
4 Boone, T. (2013). *Introduction to Exercise Physiology*. Burlington, MA: Jones & Bartlett Learning.
5 Boone, T. (2010). *Integrating Spirituality and Exercise Physiology: Toward a New Understanding of Health*. Lewiston, NY: The Edwin Mellen Press.
6 Sheila, C., Grossman, S. C., & Valiga, T. M. (2009). *The New Leadership Challenge: Creating the Future of Nursing*. Philadelphia, PA: F. A. Davis.
7 Schuller, R. A. (1987). *Power to Grow Beyond Yourself*. Old Tappan, NJ: Fleming H. Revell Company.

5
WE HAVE A DESTINY TO FULFILL

> We must think our work is important to bring forth positive results, and if we start living as healthcare professionals, we will become our vision.

I have been very fortunate as a teacher to have my father as my inspiration on many different levels. I believe students across six colleges and universities have benefited from his thinking and influence on me. Also, I am grateful to my high school football coaches who gave me a chance to prove to others that I could make the team, and I can say the same about my high school track and baseball coaches. Their support and encouragement were invaluable.

At college, the pattern was the same. As a freshman at Northwestern State University in Natchitoches, LA, I decided to try out for gymnastics. With the right influence, we start to think that, "I can do that. I can be a gymnast." It may be the result of our parents, teachers, and/or coaches who gave us the occasional comment that enabled us to try. Regardless of where the feeling may come from, the belief that you can create your own life is important.

We don't have to be perfect. We know that we will make mistakes. But, we need the guts to try. So, what if you should fail the first time or the fortieth time? At least you are consciously trying to live your dream of something different or something better. Whether it is tackling a football player who weighs 150 lbs more than you, performing a one-arm handstand on the parallel bars, or teaching students in an anatomy class how to dissect the brachial plexus to grasp the significance of the musculocutaneous nerve and its relationship to the shoulder flexors, it is liberating to know that you do not have to be perfect. After all, life is too short to believe we are not worthy of our efforts in attaining our goals.

Living life by acting on our dreams, by trying to accomplish good things for ourselves and others, and by giving our best effort at whatever it is we believe is important is a good life. In fact, I think that is why I was able to try most things when some of my friends were too uncomfortable to try. Yet, trying is not about pleasing others or the idea of perfection. It is the courage to try, believing in yourself, making a commitment, and defining who you are by your own ideas and goals.

Understandably, no one wants to look foolish. Life is too short to not desire a better destiny for the students of exercise physiology. All that is expected of academic exercise physiologists is the willingness to grow, to change their thoughts and behaviors, and genuinely experience the professional life and live it. This, I believe is the beginning point of learning who we are, why we think certain thoughts, and step in the direction of our destiny. Thus, in this way, I ask "Who are we? Are we exercise physiologists or are we exercise scientists (i.e., if such a term actually makes sense)?"

WHO ARE WE?

Exercise physiologists have no time to lose. They need to get with the professional program today and everyday thereafter. It isn't complicated.

More than once I have concluded that academic exercise physiologists are living under the illusion that they are doing everything right, that they can rise to the top of academia by publishing one research paper after another, and that they can guarantee their credibility, recognition, and tenure by playing the role of a researcher. Without question, there is at least one thing wrong with such thinking.

No matter how much they publish, and no matter how many meetings they go to for the purpose of presenting their research, their work is lacking in the steps required to move exercise physiology from a discipline to a profession. Therefore, the students will continue to find themselves on the short end of the career stick without a job and in debt.

If exercise physiologists are to realize their purpose in society as healthcare professionals, they should support ASEP as their profession-specific organization. They should be persistent and determined in their thinking to embrace the ASEP code of ethics, accreditation guidelines, and standards of practice. This thinking is not unusual, unexpected, or complicated. Yes, it breaks with tradition, and it is obviously important with respect to new ideas to sustain our profession. Parting with the past is necessary to take charge and take control of exercise physiology, especially if exercise physiologists are going to be recognized as healthcare professionals.

Understandably, exercise physiologists have made mistakes and will make more mistakes just as it is true with every evolving profession. That is life, but the question is how shall exercise physiologists deal with their slowness in grasping the reality of their need to change? How do they become who they believe they are, yet refuse to open their eyes to what must be done to be recognized as healthcare professionals (1–7).

> Life is all about change even though we don't see it. The ASEP leaders see exercise physiology as becoming a vision of something uniquely special in healthcare.

No other healthcare profession is as prepared to administer exercise to prevent and treat chronic diseases and disabilities. It is uncomfortable to witness professionals from other fields of study to think they are as equally qualified as exercise physiologists to prescribe exercise medicine (8). Without question, other professions are credible. But that is not the point, and at the heart of this analysis is that each profession already has its purpose for existing.

So, ask yourself this question: Are you an exercise physiologist? The answer to the question may be YES. But, as strange as it sounds, why are exercise physiologists so slow to learn how to be more than researchers. Clearly, this understanding comes from more than just a matter of earning a degree in exercise physiology. It is also a physical, mental, and emotional separation from sports medicine and exercise science. It is learning to disconnect from our history with physical education, sports training, and human performance. It is acknowledging that we are teachers first and researchers second. We must grasp the significance of teaching and believing in something better for our students and for the profession of exercise physiology. This is our reality.

For certain, academic exercise physiologists must exist for more than just to feed their students to physical therapy! But, of course, reality hits home here as well. We are exercise physiologists. This is clear. Yet, we are failing to act on our behalf while allowing ourselves to be guided by non-exercise physiologists. Instead, we must rise up and dare to think differently.

> Sports medicine is not the organization of exercise physiologists. ASEP is the professional organization of exercise physiologists. We must not be lukewarm in our conviction. We must know that we know, and we must do what we believe is required of us.

Coming to terms with this point is necessary if we are to own our profession. After all, we are responsible for our actions. We must triumph over our past way of thinking by daring to be different. Naturally, there will some blemishes and difficult moments. But, remember that the effort to stand up and share the respect for who we are is critical to our integrity, our sense of wholeness, and our need to focus on behalf of the singleness of purpose, that is, the professionalization of exercise physiology.

College students deserve a good return on their financial investment. Hunter R. Rawlings (9) said, "Parents want to know, what did my daughter learn, and how does it contribute to her career?" They want the faculty to start thinking straight and to focus their attention on undergraduate education. This means that academic exercise physiologists must acknowledge their shortcomings, especially the fact that they are exercise physiology teachers and not exercise scientists. They understand that we should be proud of calling ourselves Exercise Physiologists or Board Certified Exercise Physiologists. Thus, the lesson to be learned is simple. Stop trying to be what you are not and brace all that which you are!

As exercise physiologists step away from their association with the generic organizations, they will achieve fulfillment consistent with what other healthcare professionals already know. Like life, exercise physiologists are responsible for their own happiness and success. That is why they must take responsibility for their own identity, education, and success. After all, *we become what we think, what we talk about, and what we do. If we think our work is for the right reasons, if we think that our actions will bring forth positive results, and if we start living as professionals, we will become our vision.*

So, in a nutshell, why not be bold, take charge of your life, your profession, and your future. We have a destiny to fulfill. We have mountains to climb and professional horizons to explore. Put on a happy face, a new attitude, and be in control of your battles. Mediocrity is not the norm for exercise physiologists. Board Certified Exercise Physiologists understand this thinking. They do their best whether anyone is watching or not. They do not settle for less.

Should We Expect Something Better?

Here are my disclosures, I absolutely love teaching. My best calculation indicates that as a college teacher I taught approximately 400 academic courses to more than 6,000 students. Yes, I would do it again without a blink of the eye. Yes, I did research as well. In fact, while I love doing research, it was more about getting the students involved in good research and helping them learn from it rather than being recognized as a big-time researcher. Also, I should point out that I did not do research to get promoted or tenured. All that seemed to come naturally.

To teach is to do something special between yourself and the students. It is the closest thing I know where you share with students what you know, what they must learn, and why it all makes sense to pay the high tuition dollars and living costs. We teach students who go on to teach clients, patients, and students. Yes, some students become great teachers. Others write and publish books, research articles, and some become entrepreneurs.

But, strangely enough, exercise physiologists are still letting non-exercise physiologists tell us how to think and what to do. Why it has taken so long to see the need for our own professional organization isn't hard to understand when you realize we are being pulled to the future to fulfill the goals of others. Why can't we understand that in most academic departments throughout the United States, exercise physiology is being used? Rather than existing to benefit the students, these departments exist as the door of opportunity for the academic exercise physiologists to earn a big research reputation. Don't get me wrong, I understand the need for research. But, the expression "college teaching" should not be all about "college research," which ultimately devalues teaching.

Our reality is defined by how we create ourselves. Hence, it is just a matter of time before change will take place in the curriculum (such as teaching anatomy), in the students' hands-on laboratory experiences, and in the methods that we use to evaluate and educate our clients and patients (10). The exercise physiology courses will be updated to empower the students. They will have the academic opportunity to study professionalism, professional development, business, and entrepreneurship so that they will know how to start their own exercise medicine clinic (1–7). There will be less emphasis on research and motor learning to allow for the teaching of ethics and exercise medicine concepts and application, especially from the point of view of preventing and treating chronic diseases and disabilities (8).

> Exercise physiologists have no time to lose. They need to take a chance and take control. They need to play the game of professional development with their hearts and minds.

Presently, while the teaching of entrepreneurial thinking and the ASEP reality of the future do not get the attention they should in the undergraduate programs, the ASEP leaders believe this will change as exercise physiologists learn to master the future. As George Land and Beth Jarman said, "The only risk we take with the future is not to take the risk of recreating it." Yet, since exercise physiologists are not allowing the pull of the future to be realized, this is the reason why college graduates are not confident in starting their own healthcare practice. Academic exercise physiologists should be responsible for teaching their students how to start a healthcare business, what it means to operate financially using the fee-for-service approach, and how to protect themselves against a malpractice suit? They should also be held accountable for teaching students how to evaluate a client and/or patient and, then, prescribe an exercise medicine prescription.

> Sports medicine and exercise science cannot breed and nurture the winning spirit of Board Certified Exercise Physiologists.

I understand the importance of teaching glycolysis and the Krebs cycle (6). I know why students should learn the specific steps of generating energy for muscle contraction. But, shouldn't academic exercise physiologists teach and expect their students to adhere to a code of ethics and standards of practice as well (2)? The ASEP leadership believes it is important that students think of exercise physiology as a profession and not simply as a "field" or as a "discipline." This is not the first time these ideas have been presented and it will not be the last. Just as teaching cannot be simply the repetition of words, the take home message of the undergraduate degree must be more than it is. There must be more feedback that connects the dots between students, teachers, and career opportunities.

What is common among the accredited healthcare programs such as physical therapy and athletic training is the profession-specific curriculum with course work that supports each profession, its vision, and its career expectations. This point is so important that the graduating seniors should be asked to evaluate the effectiveness of the academic course work in developing and/or keeping a career-specific job. For example, "Was the degree helpful or not? What do you think was most helpful, least helpful, and what could the department and/or faculty do better?"

What are the courses, hands-on laboratory skills and experiences, and professionalism conversations and lectures that are essential for a Board Certified Exercise Physiologist to be successful? It is important that the expected outcomes of the college education (e.g., Board Certified professional healthcare entrepreneur) define the academic curriculum. The past and present association with exercise science and sports medicine is not exercise physiology and neither can define exercise physiology.

We should expect something better and the best way to get something better is to do it ourselves. First, there is the vision, which ASEP leaders have published on the ASEP website. The vision gives us direction and reason for action to live our reality as healthcare professionals. Second, we must change from what we have become to what we should be. In the end, it is as Max DePree (11) said, "We cannot become what we need to be by remaining what we are."

Final Thoughts

We must identify, talk about, and promote the profession of exercise physiology. We cannot lose the opportunities that are afforded to us with the founding of the American Society of Exercise Physiologists. This means that we should not let our skills and knowledge be taken from us by non-exercise physiologists. In the end, we are responsible for who we are and what we become. As Mahatma Gandhi (12) said, "We must become the change we want to see." So, ask yourself the following questions:

1. Are you happy being yourself?
2. Do you like being called by different titles?
3. Do you love being an exercise physiologist?
4. Are you happy being a member of a generic organization?
5. Are you glad that ASEP is part of exercise physiology?
6. Can you understand that change is a lifetime of work?
7. Can you understand that generic organizations are not interested in changing?
8. Are you willing and happy to be part of the ASEP process of change?
9. Professionalism is real, and it is necessary ... right?
10. Are you happier that you are living as a winner?
11. How does being a Board Certified Exercise Physiologist feel?

What are you thinking after reading the questions? If you are a professor, if you place your attention on publishing and research, you will have both. If you place your attention on helping your students, your mind will create that reality too. If you are a healthcare professional, are you happy serving others?

Each of us is created for a reason. A career is both personal and a necessity. It has meaning and purpose, especially when one's education makes a difference in our lives and that of our clients and patients. Thus, it is more than reasonable to conclude that college teachers who fail to appreciate this point are in violation of their duty to empower others.

If you are a college teacher, I challenge you to make teaching your priority. For certain, I believe your thinking will change when you take time to consider your destiny. Why not make your life and message count by embracing the ASEP vision of unity and the power of self-regulation to benefit our profession? Why not dedicate your work and time to helping students fill themselves with the passion of practicing exercise medicine? Why not dream of the possibilities that our own professional organization provides, and it will happen! The new world of exercise physiologists awaits us.

References

1 Boone, T. (2001). *Professional Development of Exercise Physiology*. Lewiston, NY: The Edwin Mellen Press.
2 Boone, T. (2005). *Exercise Physiology: Professional issues, organizational concerns, and ethical trends*. Lewiston, NY: The Edwin Mellen Press.
3 Boone, T. (2006). *Exercise Physiology as a Career: A guide and sourcebook*. Lewiston, NY: The Edwin Mellen Press.
4 Boone, T. (2007). *Ethical Standards and Professional Credentials in the Practice of Exercise Physiology*. Lewiston, NY: The Edwin Mellen Press.
5 Boone, T. (2009). *The Professionalization of Exercise Physiology: Certification, accreditation, and standards of practice of the American Society of Exercise Physiologists (ASEP)*. Lewiston, NY: The Edwin Mellen Press.
6 Boone, T. (2014). *Introduction to Exercise Physiology*. Burlington, MA: Jones & Bartlett Learning.
7 Boone, T. (2015). *Professionalism in Exercise Physiology*. Lewiston, NY: The Edwin Mellen Press.
8 Boone, T. (2016). *ASEP's Exercise Medicine Text for Exercise Physiologists*. Beijing, China: Bentham Science Publishers.
9 Rawlings, H. R. (2012). Why Research Universities Must Change. Inside Higher Education. (Online). www.insidehighered.com/views/2012 /03/30/essay-research-universities-must-pay-more-attention-student-learning.
10 Boone, T. (2017). *Anatomy: A pressing concern in exercise physiology*. Beijing, China: Bentham Science Publishers.
11 DePree, M. (2004). *Leadership Is an Art*. New York: Crown Publishing Company.
12 Gandhi, M. (Online). http://thinkexist.com/quotation/we_must_become_the_change_we_want_to_see/11442.html.

6
COURAGE IS ESSENTIAL

With a few exceptions, I believe "taking a stand" is a way of saying that "I agree or disagree" with what a person said. It is another way to say, "I will commit to the idea" or "I can't take a position on that." The courage to commit to a new way of thinking isn't easy. For many people, it is almost impossible to take a new position on any idea that runs counter to status quo. They are uncomfortable thinking for themselves or taking a stand on an issue. Why? The answer isn't complicated. What if your colleagues make fun of your new idea? This troubling reality is compounded by the simple fact that most people want to be liked and/or accepted by their friends and colleagues.

A "paradigm shift" takes place when there is a significant change in the way an individual (such as me or you) or a group (e.g., exercise physiologists) perceives something, and the old way of thinking (i.e., paradigm) is replaced by a new way of thinking or a new belief. As an example, I used to think ACSM was an exercise physiology organization? Later, I changed my thinking and replaced the old way of thinking with the new ASEP way of thinking. This means that I think exercise physiology is a healthcare profession and not a research discipline. Hence, if I say to you that we must change how we think, you should understand my commitment to turning the academic degree into a profitable career that is based on professionalism and professional development.

As to professional unity and the need for self-regulation, a choice confronts exercise physiologists at all levels. Will they continue thinking as they have always done for decades? Or, will they support the changes described by ASEP? The latter is the right step forward for exercise physiology. It is the 21st century paradigm shift (i.e., opportunity) to participate in the growth of a new healthcare profession. All that is necessary is to have the courage to believe you can do it.

The Courage to Create

It takes courage to face up to what exercise physiology has become and to deal with its shortcomings. Where is the courage to make a difference? Surely, there are academic exercise physiologists who are willing to take risks to change exercise physiology for the better. The one thing we need is the courage to act. Yet, more often than not, Rollo May is right when he said in *The Courage to Create*, "The most prevalent form of cowardice in our day hides behind the statement 'I did not want to get involved'" (1).

It takes courage to join ASEP. It takes courage to invest in the new view of exercise physiology. It takes courage to stay the course, to solve the transitional problems, and to manage the change process. Self-actualization is not easy. This is evident by the fact that academic exercise physiologists have avoided talking and/or writing about professionalism and/or the need for their own professional organization. The fear of being mistreated by their colleagues is powerful, which is a curious paradox for educated individuals.

The fact that some exercise physiologists are willing to challenge status quo allows for creative thinking and the hope of something better. Change takes place when people put to use the powers of their subconscious mind. It has nothing to do with academic accomplishments or a popular organization. It is as simple as saying, as we grow older we see life and our work differently. We also learn to acknowledge that we have been walking in the wrong direction sooner rather than later. It is then we understand that it is imperative to stop surrendering who we are to our fears.

Whatever side of the fence you find yourself, there is a profound importance in knowing that being open to change gives hope to our destiny. This is not a minor point. Each of us must do what we believe is important for all exercise physiologists. We must be true to ourselves and our dreams. This thinking brings something new to the profession of exercise physiology, and it should be appreciated at all levels. The act itself defines who among us is exercising self-control and, therefore, who is helping to fulfill the 21st century ASEP vision.

The power of the mind to bring forth our desired reality is incredible. It is amazing but true that the act of exercise physiologists bringing into being a new healthcare profession isn't something that is done on weekends or with an occasional moment of reflection here and there. It is a constant mental focus, an emotional faith, and a physical encounter that drives the management of change. To be sure, it is passion for an idea that something better is possible for the students of exercise physiology and the recognition of all exercise physiologists as healthcare professionals.

The ASEP ideas constitute a compelling vision that we are linked to an instinctive and genuine breakthrough as the key health professionals to prescribe exercise medicine. But by virtue of sharing a common purpose to build and unite a profession, it is clear that a major mental effort, openness, trust, respect, and emotional commitment are required by all exercise physiologists. While this point may not be a new revelation, it nonetheless requires courage, cooperation, and daily commitment to reach the ASEP goals and objectives.

If you are a believer in ASEP, why not share your thoughts with whomever to encourage creative thinking that will bring forth future possibilities of growth and change in exercise physiology? Why not help your students and colleagues realize the power in creating new solutions, perhaps, in accordance with the following statement?

> You are what you think. If you continue to think the way you always have, nothing is going to change. But, if you achieve a higher level of thinking, things will change, and you will have achieved it by your new way of thinking.

Regardless of your position or where you live, you can make a difference in the work that must be done. Help your colleagues fix their thoughts on what is right for the profession of exercise physiology by:

1. Communicating to the academic administration the need for support to fulfill the ASEP goals, thus giving shape and hope to exercise physiology.
2. Daring to engage in the necessary work, decisions, and struggles to realize the joy of participating in an organization of healthcare professionals who are driven to make sense out of the nonsense of present-day status quo.
3. Embracing the newness and the healthcare possibilities of the ASEP vision and perspective by becoming a member.
4. Supporting the ASEP originality and expression of freer professional creativity than allowed with present-day conformity.
5. Considering what it means to be guided by a code of ethics, accreditation standards, board certification, and standards of professional practice.
6. Putting aside time to study the basic structure of ASEP and its symbolic discourse of passion and commitment.
7. Disclosing the reality of problems with the existing undergraduate degree programs and generic certifications?
8. Acknowledging in conversation and writing the chaos and complexity of engaging new ideas that drive the change process.
9. Researching the capacity to imagine, to doing new things, and to experience the power in a unified professional organization.
10. Finding the time to share with friends and colleagues the fundamental harmony between an academic degree and career opportunities.

THE RIGHT ATTITUDE TO PRESS ON

Change is the reality of life. It is an immutable fact of life.

Given the circumstances exercise physiologists are faced with, a positive attitude helps to press on. By positive, I mean the right attitude that allows for optimism and less negative thoughts to do what has to be done. That is one reason why ASEP members have adopted a constructive way of viewing the change process. They see the need to get with changing "what is" to "what can be" sooner than later.

That is why ASEP endorsed the "Official Credo of an Exercise Physiologist" (2), which states that:

> *I do not choose to be a trainer, instructor, technician, or a common exercise practitioner. It is my right to be uncommon—my right to be a professional exercise physiologist. I seek professionalism and credibility, not the easy road. I do not wish to be certified by a non-exercise physiology organization that has nothing to do with the professional development of exercise physiology. I want to belong to the American Society of Exercise Physiologists. I want to be a member of the professional team of exercise physiologists as healthcare professionals. I understand the importance of a professional code of ethics, academic accreditation, ASEP board certification for exercise physiology prepared candidates, and standards of professional practice. I refuse to give away exercise physiology to non-exercise physiologists. I will not trade my education or my dignity for a non-exercise physiology major. It is my heritage and right to stand apart from non-exercise physiologists. I am proud of my membership in the American Society of Exercise Physiologists. I am proud to be a healthcare professional. I understand the importance of thinking and acting with integrity and credibility. All this is what it means to me to be an exercise physiologist.*

One of the greatest messages of ASEP is that it exists solely for exercise physiologists, regardless of the necessity to go against the conventional thinking. The ASEP leaders committed themselves to bringing into being the evolution of exercise physiologists as healthcare professionals. Part of this process is their total commitment to the ASEP vision that undergirds professionalism in exercise physiology. This means thinking as an ASEP professional member and creating something that has never existed before. It is not an easy thing to do, which is what almost every person experiences when it comes to changing.

But, there is a time when change is imperative and marks the path. It may be a feeling that something isn't right. It may be the result of having read the views of an ASEP exercise physiologist who published a paper in *Professionalization of Exercise Physiology* online electronic journal. Either way, it is a matter of time and alignment with ASEP that exercise physiologists will embrace the right attitude because they will come to understand who they are and what they do. After all, as Florence S. Shinn said in *The Game of Life and How to Play It*, "… man can only be what he sees himself to be, and only attain what he sees himself attaining."

Although seldom understood, the fact that the ASEP leaders and members believe in the change process means it is just a matter of time and the impact of their work will become a new reality that cannot be ignored.

While it may seem impossible for non-doctorate exercise physiologists to make headway within the healthcare system in United States, it is not impossible to create what never has been. The ASEP members have demonstrated their willingness to promote the healthcare reality. They understand it is important to be involved, and as such their work and commitment have helped in promoting exercise physiologists as exercise medicine professionals.

As a college teacher for more than four decades, my faith was always strong that the academic degree should make sense. That was true during my first 20 years of teaching, but interestingly it was my second 20+ years of teaching that profoundly influenced me. I was worried and frustrated with my colleagues who would not engage in a conversation about a new way to think of being an exercise physiologist. You could see it in their face, body posture, and comments. Sports medicine was their only way then and it is still true today.

They would say to me,

> I graduated with a doctorate degree from a research institution from which I call myself an exercise physiologist. Aside from my physiology courses, I was taught the importance of research and presenting at national and regional meetings. I knew that if I did research it would help me to feel good about my degree choice. I am somebody. I am recognized by other researchers. The more I publish the better I feel about myself. That is why I spend my time doing research. Teaching is simply something I have to do and, if possible, I will do less of it.

The problems that result from the emphasis on research over teaching and professional development are huge. The way you view this point will radically influence how you see exercise physiology. The problem of failing to understand the research mentality over the credibility of an academic degree is causing major suffering for thousands of students. In my own personal search for answers, I have heard from many college graduates without jobs because of the lack of a recognized career-specific job agenda. I have either read or heard their heartbreaking stories, and the apparent lack of emotional support from the faculty of their graduating institutions.

Deep down it is reasonable to conclude the obvious: All exercise physiologists must know that something is wrong! Most people today understand the purpose of getting a college degree is to secure the opportunity of getting a credible job. Therefore, we must believe that failing to find a credible job means something is wrong in academia. Understandably, while writing about the failure of the chairs, faculty, deans, and vice-presidents does not minimize the disappointment and suffering, exercise physiologists who care must never retreat from the issues of indifference and/or organizational politics and greed.

Heartbreaking as it is, the students' disappointing results must change. In your wildest imagination, do you think that a high percentage of physical therapy graduates cannot locate a credible job following graduation? No, of course not and I believe the academic exercise physiologists must redeem themselves. How, you ask? By affirming their basic instinct that having the right attitude and doing the right thing as a "college teacher" is decades overdue. They need to fight for the students. This is an idea worth considering. Undergraduate students need the sincere help of the faculty as teachers and advisors.

Moreover, if the doctorate exercise physiologists are to triumph over their failure to be properly educated while completing the doctorate degree, they must start thinking for themselves. Then, they will see the necessity of upgrading the doctorate exercise physiology courses and academic degree titles to a credible exercise physiology curriculum and degree, respectively. As Robert H. Schuller said, "Beginning is half done! Get started! Winning starts with beginning!" Schuller also said in his book, *Tough Times Never Last, But Tough People Do!* "when you have a good idea you should not hibernate, luxuriate, commiserate, procrastinate, and then you can become the person you want to be!"

Who Is in Charge?

I would like to think that my work is under my direction and not someone else. But, of course there is usually a person in charge of this and that project. It could be a chairperson, manager, director, or designated boss. Regardless, most of us understand the importance of working with our colleagues. We do so even when we believe our dreams may be significantly different from their expectations.

I understand commitment to a dream isn't easy, regardless of its importance. I understand the importance of taking a risk, especially if it will help achieve ASEP goals and objectives (3). I have also worked hard to conquer the fear of failure. Understandably, the change process is not just a challenge but several mental marathons one after the other, decade after decade.

"Never stop believing" is a phrase that I hear myself saying. "Never quit" and "stay the course" are two more phrases I say to myself to help in pulling my own strings. It seems that everything depends on a person's attitude and values. Some mornings I catch myself saying: "I am going to think positive and be happy today." Or, "Today, I believe more exercise physiologists will dare to get rid of their past way of thinking and join ASEP to make a difference." Understandably, being willing to make waves by helping to grow an organization is not easy. I can honestly say that when I posted the first-ever ASEP website in 1997, I did not realize the discipline that it would require to inspire and minister to exercise physiologists.

I also know that if I fail to do my best, I cannot help others gain fulfillment, peace of mind, and joy they need for success in their lives. Working together is not for the sake of rebellion, but rather to become our dream. This thinking is important because it adds self-esteem to individuals who are confronted with challenges that have rendered them with the wrong attitude if not indifference and a sense of defeat. Do you dare to give yourself permission to be you?

Those of us who get this point have come together under the flag of ASEP that builds positive self-esteem. It takes great courage to live in accordance with your inner thinking. I dare you to allow yourself the mental freedom to grow and to question status quo. I dare you to join the American Society of Exercise Physiologists. I dare you to challenge the old sports medicine assumptions and decide that you too can be successful, happy, and self-sufficient while helping to grow the profession of exercise physiology. The underlying message is making waves and going into uncharted waters are both critical to defining and living your own thoughts and dreams.

The failure of academic exercise physiologists to take the time to think about the necessity and the significance of the ASEP code of ethics and professionalism documents is problematic, but they can *learn from it* by joining ASEP. The truth is that publishing another research paper cannot correct the problem of failed leadership. Many college professors might think so, but here again they fail to understand what other healthcare professionals know because they have closed their minds to the full bloom of the importance of their own professional organization. In the end, the growth of exercise physiology depends on one's courage to develop the right state of mind that begins with curiosity and a passion for letting go of the old ways.

Others may disagree with Rollo May. That is fine. I don't expect everyone to get past their conformity and jump into the ASEP boat. Many people are simply scared of leaving the shore (i.e., experiencing change). Others like it as it is. They aren't interested in knowing how it could be or how it will be. Then, there is the issue of organizational politics, power, and greed. Yes, there is a strong current of "who is more powerful and bigger" in organizations throughout the United States. Perhaps a slight alteration in Neil Armstrong's famous line, "One small step for man, one giant leap for mankind" will offer hope, well-being, and opportunity for a better life regardless of the size of non-exercise physiology organizations.

Final Thoughts

Think with me for a moment: You can earn an exercise science degree and call yourself an exercise physiologist, right? No. It is unethical to refer to yourself as an exercise physiologist without earning an exercise physiology degree. Yet, it is also common for college graduates even with a kinesiology degree to refer to themselves as an exercise physiologist. It happens so often that it almost comes across as acceptable.

But, while it might seem contradictory, it could be true and yet it cannot be true unless the person with an exercise science or kinesiology degree sits for the ASEP Board Certification exam and passes it with a minimum of 70%. Then, the person who passed the exam can refer to him- or herself as an exercise physiologist or, more specifically, as an ASEP Board Certified Exercise Physiologist. This opportunity exists because so many of the academic exercise physiologists have not let go of status quo, which keeps their students on the outside looking in.

> As a profession, we have arrived with ASEP. We have defined our Code of Ethics. We have a Standards of Practice. We have our own body of knowledge unique to exercise physiologists. In time, exercise physiology will be recognized as a healthcare profession.

College students must learn to be in charge of their own destiny. All they need is a strong dose of persistence to sit for the ASEP-EPC exam to open the door of opportunity! The ASEP leaders have provided this opportunity because it the right thing to do for the students. However, in time the door will close and only the college graduates with an exercise physiology degree will qualify to sit for the EPC exam.

Swami Vivekananda said it this way, "Take up one idea. Make that one idea your life—think of it, dream of it, and live on that idea. Let the brain, muscles, nerves, every part of your body, be full of that idea, and just leave every other idea alone. This is the way to success. That is the way great spiritual giants are produced." For the graduating student, that one idea can be the EPC exam. Why not make Board Certified Exercise Physiologist your life by becoming an ASEP member? Think about it, dream about it, and live the ASEP reality of becoming a professional exercise physiologist. Get involved in the actual work of ASEP. Why?

As Swami pointed out, it isn't complicated. It is the way to the exercise physiologists' success in the healthcare profession. You don't need to fall back on the past way of thinking. Your choices are based on your purpose in life and the ASEP vision of something better for all exercise physiologists. After all, making the world a better place to live according to the shared ASEP values is a worthy goal. Also, it will help you be a happy participant in making the college degree a much better place to prepare for a lifetime of work as an exercise physiologist.

References

1 May, R. (1994). *The Courage to Create*. New York: W. W. Norton & Company.
2 Exercise Physiologists: The 21st Century Healthcare Profession. (2013). Official Credo of Exercise Physiologists. (Online). https://exercisephysiologists.wordpress.com/.
3 American Society of Exercise Physiologists. (2018). ASEP Goals and Objectives. (Online). www.asep.org/index.php/about-asep/goals-objectives/.

7

THE SEARCH FOR LEADERS

There are many reasons for the existence of ASEP and its leadership. The most powerful reason is to build the future as it should be for all exercise physiologists. The fact that leadership is based on trust speaks volumes. Why aren't the academic exercise physiologists taking a stand with ASEP rather than supporting status quo? They must be aware that their students trust them to provide the best education and career opportunities. After all, integrity and honesty are not just desired qualities of a college teacher but expected as well. And yet, the ASEP leaders have had the onerous task of selling its vision to academic exercise physiologists.

While a purpose driven life is not a common topic in exercise physiology, it is nonetheless very important. The profession of exercise physiology needs leadership that thinks this way. The fact that exercise physiology is short on leadership is a clear indication of the time academic exercise physiologists spend engaged in activities with little to no serious emphasis on the students' professional development and career options (1).

Intimately tied to the pursuit of research and publishing is the recognition and career stability associated with promotion and tenure. Also, it is important to point out that college teachers are uncomfortable doing anything that might upset the administration's interest in more and more research publications.

This leaves the ASEP leaders with the responsibility to present new ideas for student careers after graduation. Fortunately, they are willing to speak up and promote professionalism in exercise physiology. But, they need other exercise physiologists who are willing to speak up and help pursue the professionalization of exercise physiology as a credible healthcare profession. If they would only take a moment and challenge the status quo, their unique talents and skills would help make exercise physiology a better academic major.

Others have experienced the same challenges, especially members of other healthcare professions. They understand it is a test of integrity. They figured out that change comes from within. College teachers must learn to be more involved in the students' potential for success. They need to open their eyes and minds to the possibilities of new thinking and new career opportunities. Should their thinking go against status quo, saying what you feel is part of the American dream. Sure, there will be those who criticize and say this and that, but that is just their opinion. Their pride clouds their thinking.

> True leaders in exercise physiology think for themselves.

It is important to be better than we have been for the past six or seven decades. This means being willing to talk about topics that are seldom discussed, living a dream that is different from today, and promoting change that is often complex and even awkward. Such is life when you are living a vision rather than being led by non-exercise physiology individuals who are not helping exercise physiologists. This is true even though your colleagues may never get the importance of following a different path (2).

Being a Leader

Each of us must become our own leader. Remember, as Goethe said, "Whatever you can do, or dream you can, begin it. Boldness has genius, power, and magic in it." We must embrace our purpose, vision, and shared values and do whatever is necessary to create a different future for all exercise physiologists. Yes, time is critical to helping the students of exercise physiology, and it is pastime to support the building of the profession of exercise physiology.

Remember that it is not possible to please everyone, especially the leaders of other organizations. There will be resistance. Colleagues may do what they can to make your life uncomfortable, especially if they are not willing to take risks to improve exercise physiology. They understand that organizations are supported by men and women with the desire to achieve that which is triggered by the politics of personal interest and/or gain.

Often times, they will tell you not to take it so personally. But, honestly, how is that possible when the future of your students is diminished. Students depend on the integrity of their teachers and the academic system to do what is right. That is why students do not expect to be manipulated, used, and/or dismissed. Yet, the everyday circumstances within the college environment are consistent with students being played like a puppet.

Ask yourself this question, "If exercise physiologists are not interested in teaching, why do they become college teachers?" The answer is because they are compelled to do research. That is what they were taught while working on their doctorate degree. They were willing then and still are today to believe that success comes from publishing research papers. The administrative emphasis on writing grants and research papers says to the professors that teaching is given just like faculty service.

Strange as it might sound, such thinking is consistent with the faculty members' doctorate education. They were taught the specifics of research because that is where the rewards exist. They were not taught how to teach, and they were not taught the value or importance of teaching. Thus, it is natural for them to place all their energy and time on research and publishing.

The "researchers" expect to rise to a higher level of academia by getting involved with research projects and doing what they can to be part of the publishing process. Of course, it does not have to be that way. College work can be about all three expectations: teaching, research, and service! That was in fact the original idea, but in reality, the faculty always fails at two of the three. But, as long as they publish their research papers in high impact factor journals, they are given a pat on the back. Therefore, as such, the "college teacher" is actually a "college researcher." In many academic settings, adjuncts do most of the teaching!

Over the past 20 years, I have asked myself more than once why do I assume the responsibility of trying to get rid of the holes and bumps in college teaching? It is not an easy task and, although seldom talked about, every college teacher is grateful for having a job. But, after getting the academic job, there is little to no thinking about the students and their desire for credible work after college, a good salary to raise a family, and personal and professional success. Instead, what the students hear from academic advisors is this: "When you graduate this spring, complete an application for physical therapy." From their point of view, exercise physiology is a research discipline. In fact, it is enormously comforting for them to dispose of teaching for an everlasting relationship with research.

Ask an academic exercise physiologist and they will say the following: "Well, you should understand that with all of our time spent on research we really don't know much about how to get a career-driven job for the students." Then, expect a colleague to enter the room and say, "I just received an email about our research article. It is accepted. We will be published authors next month. I'll send an email to the Chair?"

> Believe in your future as an exercise physiologist. Don't let anyone say otherwise, regardless of talent, position, or training. As a leader, you are in control.

After the congratulations subside, one of the faculty members says to the students, "You guys will do just fine. We will talk later. Dr. Fulkerson and I need to go to the lab right now and collect some data. Oh, by the way, complete the graduate application and check in with your advisor as the semester draws to an end." Meanwhile, the students look on while the academic exercise physiologists walk away smiling and talking about their research. Caught up in the moment of acknowledging that their manuscript is accepted, they confront a graduate student in the exercise physiology laboratory and ask him about how the data collection is going!

Students should not have to do it alone, especially when their professors tell them to spend more money on another college degree (i.e., if they are accepted in the program or otherwise they go back home to live with their parents.) The world understands this everyday outcome for thousands of students, and that is why the seed of positive interaction between the two explains the irrefutable need to correct status quo and put it behind us. Where is the mutual respect and honesty?

Taking Responsibility

When you take responsibility in changing your thinking, you change everything. While this may sound odd, progress requires working at a good idea. As J. Jacobson said, "A good idea is like a wheelbarrow; it will go nowhere unless you push it." Success comes to those who keep repeating the process of change to bring about the wholeness and maturity of a new idea.

> The power of being responsible as a college teacher lies in only one person and that is YOU. Are you a researcher or a teacher? It is up to every college teacher to be a teacher first and a researcher second. Remember, "You become what you say you will be."

Without question, every faculty member has the right and duty to do research. But, it is also their responsibility to create excellent teaching conditions for the students of exercise physiology. Ordinary logic quickly discounts research over teaching. Thus, it is time to abandon the limits placed on teaching and tap into a deeper reality that will bring out the greatness within the college professors as teachers first and researchers second.

Also, until we tap into a deeper reality that embraces the ASEP vision and meaningful changes for all exercise physiologists, we will either fail to progress accordingly or slide back into our old ways. This does not mean that exercise physiologists must walk away from doing research or even disconnect themselves from non-exercise physiology organizations. Research is important. Connecting with colleagues from other professions is important as well. But, it is imperative that research exist alongside an equal emphasis on a high quality of teaching.

To some exercise physiologists, this thinking is logical and appropriate. To the majority of exercise physiologists, this viewpoint is likely to have many negative connotations. We can choose to remain as we are, which will most likely result in no changes in the students' future, or we take responsibility for the education of our students. Remember that a faculty member does not suddenly become less important because he or she begins to demonstrate an interest in teaching and caring about the future success of his or her students. This is not a misunderstanding, it is the truth.

Leaders organize their work with positive thoughts, ideas, and people. This is especially people who believe in themselves, in possibilities, and in becoming who they think they were meant to be. Life is too short to live on your knees. Leaders are not comfortable on their knees (i.e., controlled by the behavior of others). They want to stand up and walk the walk, talk the talk, and dream the dream. It is what they are, and it is why they give and sacrifice on behalf of their dreams and expectations. They want to become who they were meant to be (3). That is why they are open to new ideas that are real and critical to doing the right thing.

No doubt you have heard that cleaning the car is John's responsibility, Keith is responsible for cutting the grass, and parents are responsible for teaching their children right from wrong. Well, life is much the same on the college campus. College teachers are responsible for helping their students to be the best they can be by being prepared to teach the most up-to-date information. Similarly, nurses are responsible for their patients, and academic physical therapists understand they are responsible for teaching about ethics and professionalism in their classes. Academic athletic trainers are responsible for teaching their students about their profession-specific code of ethics and standards of practice. It isn't a complicated thought process.

> Do you have the courage and conviction to think not only with your head, but with your heart? Do you recognize the need for excellent teaching? The need for an academic curriculum that will prepare the students for success after college? Do you feel a certain necessity to help students more so than yourself?

Academic exercise physiologists should ask themselves: "To whom are we responsible?" "What are we responsible for doing?" The ASEP leaders' response to both questions is not a complicated response. They understand the needs of the students come first. They get that if the students' job-related skills after college are not enhanced by the teaching process, the teachers should be held responsible? If teachers fail to place the proper emphasis on the measurement of VO_2 max or professionalism and ethics, then they should be held accountable?

College teachers should be held responsible for teaching profession-specific course content. Moreover, it is reasonable to conclude that if professors are responsible to their students as society expects, professors cannot place scientific research or other interests above teaching. While it is appropriate to have a great sense of responsibility for doing research, it is inappropriate to rationalize bad teaching practices due to relatively little time spent preparing for lectures. Teachers who do make excuses for their bad teaching skills may suffer from moral myopia (4).

The word "responsibility" is akin to saying, "the responsible driver" or "the responsible parent" or more to the point, "the responsible teacher." But, in reality, the image of the college teacher today is a person who spends a considerable amount of time thinking, writing, and attending to research journals on their behalf. It is time spent shaping ideas that drive research projects and publishing. It is work that benefits the teachers more than the students. It is the "home run" that benefits the "researcher" versus the "teacher."

While education has its steps of advancement and survival, faculty members believe nothing has changed or will change. They take pleasure in doing research and publishing papers and turn a deaf ear to the fact that 50% of Americans believe that the primary purpose of getting a college degree is to learn specific skills and knowledge that will be used in the workplace. Hence, professors who aren't interested in teaching are not helping their students to be successful after college. This means that if the only proof society has of academic quality is research, then, the value placed on a college degree is meaningless.

This must be true even though the desire to do research, to get promoted, and to get tenure is the "academic game" played by the college faculty. It has been and still is the reality of the academic setting. This means the driving force behind college teachers as researchers first is not in accordance with society's expectation and the students' educational need for getting a job after college. Implicit in this thinking is the responsibility of the teacher-the-helper to facilitate the students' desire to get a return on their investment.

Teaching should be first when it comes to the highest good for all students no matter what the implied argument may be otherwise. College isn't any longer about providing college graduates with an understanding of the world or developing their critical thinking abilities. That kind of leadership and thinking is not helping graduates get career-specific jobs. That is why the teaching that goes on within academia should benefit the students, especially at private universities where tuition and fees plus room and board have, in some cases, increased to more than $50,000 per year.

If exercise physiologists are to approach academia with the idea of "taking responsibility" for their students, the "college professor" would counsel themselves differently from the obvious imperfections that drive today's academic settings. The lack of emphasis on leadership and teaching must change, and the question of scientific research versus academic leadership that promotes teaching must change. Yes, it is reasonable to conclude that both can be done well, but "taking responsibility" means placing the emphasis on teaching at a higher level than the present-day emphasis on scientific research and publishing.

Final Thoughts

It is unfortunate that excellence in teaching and academic interest in career-specific leadership is viewed as a lack of commitment to scientific research. The bottom line is that college teachers cannot be encouraged or allowed to act in an isolated manner from their responsibility to meet the academic and career needs of their students. Thus, to argue that research is more important than teaching is an exploitation of the academic setting. College teachers must be responsible to their students and to society's needs. To help ensure this is the case, it is also the responsibility of the chairperson and other administrators to uphold this thinking.

Although the academic setting is the hope of something better for the college students, academic exercise physiologists are lacking in servant leadership. Matthew Henry (1662–1714), an English Presbyterian minister and writer was right when he said, "None so blind as those that will not see" (5). We, the 21st century ASEP exercise physiologists, must reach out to our colleagues to help them overcome today's thinking. We must act on the problems before us, and we must have the courage and desire to deal effectively with our fear of changing (6). Our students need more leadership in "what is exercise medicine," "how to execute the practice of exercise medicine," and how to create an "Exercise Medicine Clinic."

In 2000, the following comment was published in the *Professionalization of Exercise Physiology-online* (7):

> In the not too distance future, the PhD academic exercise physiologist, who probably knows little to nothing about entrepreneurial ventures as an emerging trend in our economy, will be expected to offer entrepreneurship courses for undergraduates and master level prepared exercise physiologists. The question is whether they will find the time to leave the laboratory to address the new opportunities in the public (service) sector. Another question is whether they will help their students develop the necessary strategic alliances with other entrepreneurs, locally and otherwise. Students who develop entrepreneurial, negotiation, and legal skills will be prepared for the 21st century.

Key Point: We should work, not with anxiety but with desire; not by putting down our colleagues but with a caring heart and kindness; not by pressure but in a state of professional recognition and receptivity. We do not have to be scare of thinking differently, but rather look forward to doing so on behalf of our students and the exercise physiology profession.

Meaningful and sustainable change means anticipating the future. It means doing the right things for the right reasons. It also means acknowledging the fact that non-exercise physiology healthcare practitioners are continuing to lead exercise physiologists in the wrong direction, which is problematic for the college students majoring in exercise physiology. These non-EP practitioners are doing what they can to keep exercise physiology as a research discipline. They do not want it to be recognized as the healthcare profession.

> We know that our thoughts are constantly changing from one idea to another. Can we not change our way of looking at exercise physiology instead of staying the same (discipline vs. healthcare profession)?

History informs us that the adage, "If it ain't broke, don't fix it" is often the expression to avoid change because everything seems to be working so well that it is too comfortable. There is no reason to change. After all, the universities are doing rather well with the undergraduate students' tuition dollars to subsidize other costly activities. The idea of changing creates tension, given the expectation and necessity to adjust to a new protocol. No one presently wants to create a new procedural process and a new way to think about students.

The bottom line is that no one is interested in fixing the problem, which appears to be why so few chairs, deans, and exercise physiologists are willing to embrace the ASEP perspective. What they will do is to continue their faculty status as they were taught and have always done because of the belief that emphasis on undergraduate instruction would hurt the research mission of academic institutions.

Unlike the faculty in other science-oriented degrees (in particular, physical therapy, athletic training, and nursing), exercise physiologists are slow to think outside the box (8). This is a problem for the students of exercise physiology. A credible education is important for the students. Leaders from different points of view should understand the urgency to do what is in the students' best interest. It should not be a question of what the faculty may lose or how hard it might be to adjust, but to simply step forward and support the change process because it will help the students.

The simple truth is that each time a student of an ASEP accredited exercise physiology degree is hired as a Board Certified Exercise Physiologist to observe, interact, and apply the exercise physiology standards of practice to prevent chronic diseases and/or disabilities it is a win for all exercise physiologist. Also, every college teacher who engages the ASEP entrepreneurial thinking and/or the risk-taking spirit to benefit their students is a vital part of the ASEP spirit of supporting and conveying the importance and recognition of exercise physiology as a healthcare profession.

References

1 Boone, T. (2001). *Professional Development of Exercise Physiologist*. Lewiston, NY: The Edwin Mellen Press.
2 American Society of Exercise Physiologists. (2017). ASEP Goals and Objectives. (Online). www.asep.org/index.php/about-asep/goals-objectives/.
3 Boone, T. (2015). *Promoting Professionalism in Exercise Physiology*. Lewiston, NY: The Edwin Mellen Press.
4 McCombs School of Business. (2014). Moral Myopia. Ethics Unwrapped. (Online). http://ethicsunwrapped.utexas.edu/video/moral-myopia.
5 Dels, R. (2015). The Bible-Related Quote That's Not in the Bible. Quote/Counterquote. (Online). www.quotecounterquote.com/2011/04/none-so-blind-as-those-that-will-not.html.

6 Boone, T. (2000). Leadership in Exercise Physiology. Professionalization of Exercise Physiology-online. (Online). www.asep.org/asep/asep/jan22.html.
7 Boone, T. (2000). The Exercise Physiologists as an Entrepreneur. Professionalization of Exercise Physiology-online. (Online). www.asep.org/asep/asep/jan2.html.
8 Boone, T. (2008). An Invitation to Think Outside the Box. Professionalization of Exercise Physiology-online. (Online). www.asep.org/asep/asep/InvitationToThink.html.

8
THINKING STRAIGHT

If you are a young person looking to enter college in a few months, you may want to ask the registrar or the department chair: "Is the exercise physiology major accredited by the ASEP organization?" The answer is very important, especially since the outstanding student loans are approaching $1.2 trillion. There is a real concern that if the academic major is not accredited, it may have a negative influence on students' education and job opportunities? Thus, it is likely the student's question is this, given that the exercise physiology degree is an accredited degree, "The exercise physiology major will provide me increased opportunities to get a credible career-specific job in the public sector, right? Great, that is what I thought."

While exercise physiology as an actual degree by title in the United States is relatively uncommon, it does exist. What is common is the majority of degree programs, such as exercise science, kinesiology, human performance, sports sciences, and others that are often considered the same as exercise physiology. While these degree programs may offer somewhat similar academic courses, they are not an exercise physiology degree.

> College professors should not be allowed to avoid getting involved with the job-related problems faced by exercise science students.

That is why the following statement or something similar to it more often than not appears on the department websites (1): "The exercise science major prepares students for leadership roles in a number of career opportunities, including clinical exercise settings and corporate and hospital wellness programs, or as personal fitness trainers, exercise specialists, and strength and conditioning coaches."

The seldom discussed truth is that most exercise science students find it difficult to get a job following graduation. They end up as personal trainers or apply to graduate school to avoid going back home to live. If only they had taken to heart the true meaning why the majority of the departments of exercise science state on their website the following: "The Health and Exercise Science degree (2) ... is designed to serve as a pre-professional degree only and does not prepare the student to enter the job market upon graduation with a bachelor's degree."

There is a tremendous amount of misinformation and confusion as to which degree programs are credible and which ones are not. Regardless of what a website says, the content may be misleading. As an example, it is incorrect and unethical for a website to say, "The exercise science degree prepares students for a career in exercise physiology." Title does matter, although it may not be obvious to the chairperson and/or faculty.

> There isn't anything wrong with a pre-professional degree program if in fact the student is interested in medical school, law, nursing, architecture, and so forth. But, if the undergraduate student is interested in exercise physiology, he or she should find an academic institution that offers the exercise physiology major.

ASEP The Future

If you are interested in exercise physiology, you should know that the American Society of Exercise Physiologists (ASEP) is the professional organization of exercise physiologists in the United States. It is the responsibility of ASEP to accredit the college level exercise physiology degree program. To date, with the help of the ASEP exercise physiologists, there are five academic departments that have converted exercise science or one of a dozen other degree programs to exercise physiology.

No doubt the process of transitioning through the inertia of past thinking will take place across 40 or more years. As I said in 2011 (3),

> Transitions are always a bit crazy. Nothing transforms easily. However, if it is desired, reorienting one's mind around the future versus the past is a matter of caring and making the most of change than just surviving. The difference between the two is huge, especially in terms of the need for change.

The ASEP leaders believe that taking responsibility for the students' education is vital to making a difference in academia. There are still many academic departments where the faculty continues to define exercise physiology as a sub-discipline of kinesiology. Obviously, from the ASEP perspective, such thinking is entirely incorrect. It is the intention and willingness of the ASEP leaders to share the inappropriateness of such thinking.

> Generic strategies are developed by generic organizations to build or maintain their competitive advantages in the competitive access of members.

Their failure to let go of the past is exactly why exercise physiologists are easy targets for several generic organizations. So, with that information, it is also imperative that exercise physiologists do what is right and necessary to transition from a research discipline to a healthcare profession. Regardless of the feelings of discomfort the transition may induce, the negative statements and attitudes of some colleagues, and the challenges ahead, it is the right thing to do. We are no longer part of the kinesiology or exercise science way of thinking. Thus, exercise physiology is ours to create.

For certain, it is pastime to exit the exercise science mentality so that exercise physiologists can become who they are meant to be. This means holding on to ASEP, taking on the challenge of changing and becoming the ASEP healthcare professionals, and contributing to society by making a distinct difference in the prescription of exercise medicine. That difference can be predicted, given the possibilities in the students' ASEP accredited education.

This thinking will help to change the lives of our students. It is called "straight thinking." It is not driven by the old dogma of the past (4). Instead, it is all about discovering the new world and life of ASEP, exercise physiology, healthcare, and entrepreneurial health related business opportunities. It is the intention of ASEP leaders to individually and collectively to open up the future of Board Certified Exercise Physiologists to exercise medicine opportunities for themselves and for society.

Now, compare the previously described new way of straight thinking to the old way of failed thinking, which is more of the same on the academic websites (5): "The exercise science concentration prepares students for graduate study in exercise science-related degrees." Really, ask yourself: Is that what the departments are all about? Is that why the students and their parents spend so much money on tuition and living fees for star research professors who rarely teach? If so, is the college degree a waste of time! And, if so, is that the reason the department's legal defense is always advising the graduating students of exercise science to complete the application to one or more of the departments of physical therapy, occupational therapy, chiropractor, and/or athletic training?

> With the cost of education increasing faster than inflation, students (and their parents) are beginning to ask, "Is it worth it?"

The beauty of exercise physiology is that it is a healthcare profession with the expertise of exercise physiologists to safely prescribe exercise medicine, particularly if they are an ASEP Board Certified Exercise Physiologist (6). This was pointed out in 2010 in an article (7) entitled "Greener Grass!" As Charles Darwin noted, "It is not the strongest of the species that survive, nor the most intelligent, but the one most responsive to change."

Can non-ASEP exercise physiologists meet the challenge of changing? I am hopeful they can. One way to motivate them away from staying stuck in the past is to provide insight and understanding of the phenomenal possibilities with the ASEP organization. Regardless of the uncharted domain of unknowns, why not read and study new viewpoints published in the ASEP professionalism journals? Why not contemplate the ASEP way of thinking about exercise physiology, and create a new view of yourself with ASEP?

Here, my point is simply this: As an exercise physiology practitioner, why not choose a path that represents greener grass. This is what Ahrens did. She is an ASEP Board Certified Exercise Physiologist. When she graduated from The College of St. Scholastica in Duluth, MN with an "exercise physiology degree," she started the Ahrens Exercise Physiology Business. In our unique era, it has made all the difference in her life and that of her family. That is also why the ASEP Accreditation Guidelines are important in the academic preparation of exercise physiologists (8). Academic accreditation helps to move college students from a paradigm of the fitness instructor or exercise specialist to a mind and body exercise medicine healthcare professional.

The ASEP leaders invite you to see what is happening in the world of regular exercise and the prevention and/or treatment of chronic diseases and disabilities. It is the exercise physiologists' hands-on healthcare business that will position them as effective leaders in prescribing exercise medicine. With a few business courses that are 100% within the students' reach while in college, the exercise physiology majors can prepare themselves as healthcare business professionals with an increased opportunity for career success.

In their healthcare business setting, exercise physiologists will meet clients on their turf instead of the traditional instructor, specialist, or trainer's gym. The ASEP leaders' point of view is that healthcare involves the biological, physical, psychological, and spiritual dimensions of a client or patient's life. It involves teaching clients about self-responsibility and awareness of cardiovascular fitness, nutritional competence, and stress management. Their improvement in health and well-being is possible with the right guidance driven by straight thinking from ASEP Board Certified Exercise Physiologists.

Not only will ASEP Board Certified Exercise Physiologists help clients and patients recover from illness and disability while improving their quality of life, exercise medicine will help; (a) decrease the cost of treating chronic diseases; and (b) will improve health and decrease the risk of all-cause mortality. Their work will help to create a new and different world of healthcare service, especially in light of the fact that only 25% of adults in United States report engaging in 30 minutes of moderate-intensity activity on five or more days per week. Fortunately, the ASEP leaders are promoting the necessary changes for survival and growth of exercise physiologists as credible healthcare providers.

Never Give Up

Hardly anyone would be an athlete without the will to try. Failure is okay as long as we get up and try again. How else would we learn whether it is sports or life? In academia, the courage it takes to speak up to upgrade an exercise science degree to an accredited exercise physiology degree isn't all that different from a gymnast who is uncomfortable with trying for the first time a full twisting double back off the high bar.

Not everyone is willing to do what it takes to be a gymnast, an athlete, an artist, or a Board Certified Exercise Physiologist. However, one thing is certain, if you don't try to be different and if you don't try to think differently about exercise physiology, you will have little to say about your future after college. Tony Robbins said, "If you do what you've always done, you'll get what you've always gotten."

How did this thinking get started in my life? It was during my senior year in high school. I was told by the speech teacher that it was my turn to do a demonstration speech. Gymnasts from Northwestern State University (NSU) in Natchitoches, LA put on an exhibition at my high school in Leesville, LA a week earlier.

> It is a laboratory hands-on experience that very few exercise physiology students have the opportunity to do ... cadaveric dissection. Yet, without time spent in dissecting, it is very much like not knowing how to collect expired gas using a metabolic analyzer to determine VO_2 max.

After watching the gymnasts perform I decided to teach myself how to do a handstand, which sparked my interest in anatomy (realizing that would be the content of my speech). I went to the Vernon Parish Library (two blocks from my home), checked out an anatomy book to teach myself the muscles of the chest and shoulders, and the rest is history. I did a handstand several times in my speech class and talked about the muscles I used to position my arms, to grasp the arms of a chair from which I did the handstand as well as the muscles I used in my lower extremities to kick up into the handstand position. I got an A on the speech and went on to become an All-American gymnast at NSU.

After coaching men's gymnastics at the University of Louisiana in Monroe, I accepted a teaching position at the University of Florida. After three years, I decided it was time to move to Tallahassee to get the doctorate degree at Florida State University (FSU). During my second year of Ph.D. work, I dissected cadavers that led me to emphasize the study of anatomy by exercise physiology students. I left FSU and accepted a job at Wake Forest University (WFU) in Winston-Salem, NC where I procured cadavers from Bowman Grey School of Medicine to develop an anatomy laboratory at WFU. Then, I accepted a position at the University of Southern Mississippi (USM) in Hattiesburg, MS. After several years there, I procured cadavers from the Department of Anatomy at the University of Mississippi Medical School in Jackson, MS to start an anatomy lab with cadavers. After I left USM, I started my third anatomy laboratory with cadavers at The College of Saint Scholastica in Duluth, MN.

The idea of having access to cadavers was so uncommon that some of my exercise physiology colleagues laughed at me, which is the first point I want to emphasize. Do not let the behavior of others get in the way of a good idea. Interestingly, when I presented the idea to several faculty members in the Anatomy Department at Wake Forest Bowman Grey School of Medicine, they thought it was a great idea. They felt that our students should have the same opportunity to learn anatomy as the physical therapy (PT), occupational therapy (OT), nursing, and other healthcare students already had throughout the United States. Anatomy is important. That is why my 2013 college textbook, *Introduction to Exercise Physiology*, has three chapters that are dedicated to anatomy (9).

> The primary objective of the EPC examination is to test the candidate's competence in the profession of exercise physiology. Such competence includes adequate academic and hands-on knowledge, the ability to apply such knowledge with good judgment, and an understanding of professional and ethical responsibility.

Aside from the usual chapters in an exercise physiology college text, there are three chapters about ASEP, exercise physiologists as healthcare professionals, and exercise medicine. Being able to talk the same anatomical language as other healthcare professionals is important for referrals, respect from clients and patients, and professional success. As healthcare professionals, we must stop limiting ourselves to just physiology, especially when the exercise physiology academic course work is so much more.

> When anatomy is not taught to exercise physiology students, there is little opportunity to understand anatomical principles and relationships. In fact, it is imperative that they have the same exposure to anatomy as other students have.

As an example, and my second point that I want to highlight, I agree with Dr. Sugarman and Lucy Freeman (10) who pointed out in their book, *The Search for Serenity* that "The body and mind are different sides of the same coin." Their thinking and authors of similar books led me to publish, *Integrating Spirituality and*

Exercise Physiology (11). I cannot help but be impressed with the power that spirituality plays in health and disease. In 1994, 17 out of 126 accredited medical schools in the United States offered courses on spirituality in medicine (12). By 2004, this number and percent (13.5%) had increased to 84 medical schools and 66.67%, respectively (13).

No doubt there is the belief that it will help the medical students become better medical doctors. I wonder with today's emphasis on exercise medicine, how many exercise physiologists are teaching in medical schools? I have to say, I do not know, but probably very few. However, my first point is, even though exercise physiologists are not teaching medical students the specifics of exercise medicine, I am confident there is no way that medicine is going to be able to stand on the sideline and ignore Board Certified Exercise Physiologists as the experts in prescribing exercise medicine.

I also believe it is only a matter of time before medical schools hire exercise physiologists. Why? Because the lack of academic courses and hands-on exercise physiology laboratory experiences specific to exercise testing, prescription, and medicine in the existing medical curricula makes it difficult for the medical doctors to discuss exercise medicine and/or take on the role of the ASEP Board Certified Exercise Physiologists as healthcare professionals.

Researcher or Teacher

There is intense pressure on college professors to bring in grants and publish research papers to get tenured. That is why professors spend their time collecting data and writing manuscripts. Graduate students and adjunct professors do the majority of the undergraduate teaching. Recently, I read the following statement (14): "The faculty in our PhD program in Exercise Physiology is ranked 7th across the U.S. by the Chronicles of Higher Education. This ranking is based on research publications, research citations, and federal funding for our graduate faculty."

While research is important, why didn't the ranking process also consider the faculty's commitment and/or quality of teaching? Maybe, part of the answer is because it is common knowledge that the faculty with a strong emphasis on research brings praise to the department while outstanding teachers with an average research record do not get tenure. While it may not be openly talked about among college faculty, it is understood that teaching is secondary. No doubt this point of view is a major reason that approximately 70% of the faculty in some colleges and universities are adjunct teachers who are paid an average of $2,500 per course without health benefits (15).

It is clear that academic institutions are businesses driven by the number of research papers published by the faculty, more so than an academic environment that drives a higher level of critical thinking skills and credible career options for the students. Yet, strangely enough to the ears of the faculty, as Sarah Kendzoir (16) said, "Academic publishing is no guarantee of anything, except possibly the paywalled obsolescence of your work."

This doesn't mean publishing has no value. Teaching what is known without producing new ideas that surface from research is not the answer. Good research clarifies and reshapes our understanding of important topics, and it can help save lives. What it cannot do is get the college graduates a job, and this is my point even if students are working on a master's degree. Also, however difficult it is to accept, what if I said to you that it is very likely that a great many research papers are not read by anyone other than authors, referees, and journal editors. While disappointing for sure, the greater problem is failure to emphasize the quality of the students' education and specifics about credible career options after college.

> By thinking as a leader who is willing to embrace and support the students of exercise physiology, you will be in a better position to communicate a vision and strategy that is both flexible and yet specific to make the impossible happen today rather than later.

The conformity of the exercise physiology faculty to the exercise science degree title and course work is the number one problem faced by exercise physiologists. Why aren't the academic exercise physiologists asking the question: "Why settle for the exercise science degree title and not the exercise physiology degree title?" More than once, I have been told, "because that is the way it has always been." Also, I have heard many times that, "You need a master's degree to be a clinical exercise physiologist," and others have said, "You need the Ph.D. to be an exercise physiologist."

In fact, a Ph.D. exercise physiologist said to me that: "Just because your students graduate with an academic degree in Exercise Physiology, you cannot allow them to refer to themselves as an Exercise Physiologist with just an undergraduate degree." Her comment was shocking to me. Without blinking, I just looked at her. If thinkers lead with their minds as I have heard often in academia, I can only say that it is likely she had not experienced an original idea in her academic life for fear of not being accepted by her status quo colleagues.

Equally troubling is the unanalyzed title, "clinical exercise physiologist" as though it is different from the title, "exercise physiologist." Such thinking must be the result of lazy minds that seldom stop to consider whether their actions are appropriate or correct. The fact that all exercise physiologists are educated to work with both "a clinical population and/or a healthy population" demonstrates the misplaced thinking of the accepted status quo.

The idea of a distinction between the two titles is thinking caught in decades of failed rhetoric and misplaced politics of a generic organization, which reminds me of the rather popular misinterpretation and description of the undergraduate degree, which is: "The Bachelor of Science program is a preparatory program for graduate or professional school in areas such as exercise physiology, physical therapy, or medicine." In other words, the undergraduate degree is not designed to connect the college graduate to a career in healthcare. Rather, the BS degree is a preparatory degree plan, which means the students are not getting an academic degree that has future career opportunities!

Honestly, can you believe what you read? Vision demands a high price! The misguided thinking, hurtful comments, and the darkness of a colleague's opinions linger for decades. If we are willing to pay the price for the ASEP vision, share in its commitment to ideas, goals, and values that will help to improve the profession of exercise physiology, then the primary concern is not being part of a big crowd of people from 10 or more different disciplines and/or professionals, but to be with and create a professional relationship with ASEP exercise physiologists.

> As a leader in exercise physiology, communicate to others why you think the ASEP Board Certification is making things happen, part of which is overseeing the new reality of exercise medicine and related healthcare opportunities.

Here is a big and powerful idea, and it isn't that complicated. Why not update the exercise science degree in the 3,000+ colleges and universities to the ASEP accredited exercise physiology degree? Why not unify these programs by assigning one degree title to them, that is, the exercise physiology degree title? Then, we can acknowledge that we are all exercise physiologists and not the title, exercise scientists (whatever that means since there isn't an academic degree with that title). Moreover, why not teach our students from undergraduate level through the doctorate degree the importance of professionalism, professional development, and ASEP exercise physiology-specific code of ethics, academic accreditation, board certification, and standards of practice?

In light of what has been said, no wonder the doctorate student graduates with the belief that research is the only thing that is important? It is strange to say but true that there are very few leaders in exercise physiology who teach about professionalism at the doctorate level. College professors are researchers. To the surprise of the parents and students, they are not teachers.

Also, strangely enough, there is limited to no discussion of leadership or ethical teaching at the doctorate level. Hence, after completing the Ph.D. degree, Dr. Albert said: "If I want to I can refer to myself as a sports nutritionist even though my degree is in kinesiology?" Dr. Bart asked Dr. Oz a sports nutrition question: "Should I teach sports supplements (given the likelihood of getting a big grant) or just sports nutrition?" Other academic exercise physiologists are wrestling with the decision to teach the physiological and metabolic benefits of steroids or the specifics of ethical training practices? The end result is confusion and misguided thinking when professors want to be a good teacher were not taught how to teach or the ethics of the course content.

Perhaps the reason many exercise physiologists do not change (i.e., think outside the box) is because they do not dare to be different, which raises the question: "What does being different mean?" The answer is:

- Not being afraid to challenge the norm;
- Being willing to take a chance;
- Asking why;
- Acting as a change agent;
- Charting your own destiny; and
- Having the audacity to consider new realities.

Being different is about "believing in yourself" and "living your dream." It was Debbie Millman (17) who said, "If you imagine less, less will be what you undoubtedly deserve." Less is definitely what the students of exercise physiology are getting when the mind of the professors is set on doing research. This means the academic exercise physiologists who expected a different academic setting must not stop until students get what they deserve, regardless of the departmental status quo and/or colleagues who are not willing to change and focus on the needs of their students.

The take home message is work as hard as you can at growing the profession of exercise physiology. Imagine and think of your students as future healthcare professionals. Do not allow yesterday's thinking to compromise your feelings or ideas, and do not waste time with colleagues who are not willing to share in the personal responsibility of promoting and developing professionalism in exercise physiologists. Stay the course and do it again tomorrow and every day thereafter.

The ASEP members believe there is more to academia, the college degree, and the profession of exercise physiology than present-day thinking. For certain, the college experience does not exist simply as a pre-professional preparation for physical therapy or nursing. The members anxiously look forward to the day that teaching promotes ideas and new thinking that will help exercise physiologists come together as healthcare professionals. That day means exercise physiologists will no longer do what is common or what is expected of them by the generic organizations. Instead, the ASEP members will ask the questions: "What can we do to take charge of exercise physiology as a healthcare profession?" "What can we do to empower our students and contribute to the well-being of society?"

> By thinking as an ASEP Board Certified Exercise Physiologist, you will be in a better position to make the impossible happen.

But as time goes on, the trouble is that unless more academic exercise physiologists get involved with ASEP, more students will find themselves after college as personal trainers or fitness instructors. No one should have to default to becoming a trainer unless that is what they want to do and if that is the case, then a college degree may not be necessary. If so, stop paying thousands of dollars in college tuition fees and other costs and put the money into a fitness business?

Life is short. If you do not like something, you must do what you can to change it. Living your dream is 100% better than working on behalf of another person's self-interest. I would like to say to the skeptics, that is, those of you who are likely to say, "Oh, what a loser the author is! He'll get over it, and then he'll be just like everyone else." No! Not true. No way. I am here to stay the course. ASEP is here to stay! I am living my dream right now.

We in ASEP have the desire, strength, will, and determination to ride it out to the end because "*We dare to be different*." It is up to you to make the decision of your life. So, go ahead and ask the forbidden questions and search out the right answers for you. If you have ever had dreams of leadership, now is the time to get involved with the ASEP organization. As a beginning point, ask yourself the following questions:

1. Do you have the courage to be different? Remember, if you think you can, there is an excellent chance you will.
2. Do you have desire and willingness to be part of the social change process that is creating what never has been by changing and transforming exercise physiology into a true profession of the highest integrity and competence?
3. Do you have the commitment to follow the path to professional success as an exercise physiology healthcare professional?
4. Are you ready to collaborate and coach on behalf of others to understand the importance of having their own professional organization?
5. Do you feel happier knowing that you are doing something important for your family, yourself, and your clients and/or patients?

We must believe in who we are, what we do, how we do it, where we do it, and why we support the ASEP exercise physiology standards of professional practice. Understandably, forming a professional identity across such diverse divides as exercise physiology, exercise science, sports science, kinesiology, bioenergetics, human performance, health science, health and wellness, physical education, and dozens of other degree titles will not be an easy task, but it can be done. What is important is know who you are, what you care about, and what you want to see accomplished in your life.

Making a Difference

No doubt you know that change happens very slowly student by student, teacher by teacher, and decade by decade. But, always remember that every small change is still a change in the right direction. Purposeful change can make a difference. We can help exercise physiologists who are paralyzed by their fear of disapproval from colleagues and personal doubts. It will not be easy, but we must try by talking with them and by sharing our bottom line expectations in an atmosphere of trust and open communication. By being open and seeking to co-create with others we will share the ASEP message that we will change, or we will cease to exist as we should be. By this, I believe it is possible that we will wake up one morning and ask ourselves the following questions:

1. Am I a sports or physical activity person?
2. Is it health that I am interest in or is it fitness or, perhaps, athletics?
3. Is it right to say, "exercise is medicine" or "medicine is exercise" or "exercise medicine" and why?
4. Am I a lifestyle medicine professional and, if so, is that the same as having earned the exercise physiology-specific exercise medicine credential?
5. Why is it that so many exercise physiologists resist joining ASEP?
6. Is ACSM an exercise physiology organization and, if not, why am I still a member?
7. What are the differences between a personal trainer certification and the ASEP Board Certification?
8. Do exercise physiologists need their own code of ethics, accreditation guidelines, board certification, and standards of professional practice, as presented by the ASEP profession-specific organization?
9. Is it logical that the dozens of different exercise physiology "look alike" degree titles should continue, or should they undergo serious curriculum and philosophical changes to become the exercise physiology degree?
10. If the greatest barrier to change is the ego as most people believe, then, if academic exercise physiologists would suspend their thoughts, ideas, and opinions they would come to believe the ASEP impossibility is believable and liberating?

As Theodore M. Hesburg said, "The very essence of leadership is that you have to have a vision. It's got to be a vision you articulate clearly and forcefully on every occasion. You can't blow an uncertain trumpet." The truth is that we have isolated ourselves from a collective vision of career opportunities that will allow exercise physiologists to grow as professional exercise medicine healthcare practitioners. This means we will continue to marginalize our students if we don't come together with our unique skills and talents. Others see this as well, and they are taking advantage of the exercise physiologists' lack of collective purpose, perspective, knowledge, and service.

Understandably, the path of change and the work of challenging new ideas are neither easy nor clear. At times, inventing the future requires giving up friends and, most certainly, we create enemies. Yet, it is still a path worth taking. When exercise physiologists dare to be different, their chance of living the future of a healthcare entrepreneur is greatly increased. Dare to speak your heart and you will empower others. Dare to manage your dream of something better. Remember, we become what we think about! Why not think of yourself as an exercise physiologist or as a future ASEP Board Certified Exercise Physiologist with the credibility to start your own Exercise Medicine Clinic?

Do you realize The United States Bureau of Labor Statistics (18) states that the employment of exercise physiologists is projected to grow 13% from 2016 to 2026, which is faster than the average for all occupations? Do you know The United States Bureau of Labor Statistics identifies Exercise Physiology as a healthcare profession? To be specific, the Bureau states the following: "Exercise physiologists are nationally recognized as practitioners who provide an important and credible healthcare service to the public sector."

> Professionalization will lead to an enhance assemblage of knowledge about legitimate reasons for the exercise physiologists' interrelatedness with all health-fitness-rehabilitative care.

Now that exercise is recognized as medicine for sick patients, why is the lack of regular exercise the fourth leading cause of global mortality, illness, and suffering from chronic diseases? The short answer is that regardless of age and gender, society is both lazy and nonbelievers in the use of regular exercise to improve quality and duration of life.

Board Certified Exercise Physiologists can help prevent the premature aging, which is remarkable news to adults of all ages. The "Exercise Medicine Prescription" can help: (a) reduce mortality and the risk of recurrent breast cancer by approximately 50%; (b) decrease the risk of colon cancer by over 60%; (c) reduce the risk of developing Alzheimer's disease by approximately 40%; (d) reduce the incidence of heart disease and high blood pressure by approximately 40%; (e) lower the risk of stroke by approximately 30%; (f) lower the risk of developing type 2 diabetes by approximately 60%; and (g) decrease depression as effectively as Prozac or behavioral therapy (19).

I am convinced that if we continue exercise physiology in accordance with the 20th century exercise science thinking, it is a sure means of sacrificing our future as exercise physiology healthcare practitioners and that of our students as exercise medicine professionals. To highlight this point, Matthew Wattles, the 2004–2005 ASEP President, said 14 years ago in an article that was published in the *Professionalization of Exercise Physiology-online* (20): "The sad fact is exercise physiologists have no sense of themselves, no sense of a profession." We need people to step forward with a vision; one that will create a dynamic and sustainable Profession of Exercise Physiology.

- A profession that all exercise physiologists can be proud of and eager to share with their family, friends, and society.
- A profession that our college graduates will get the respect they have all worked so hard to achieve.
- A profession that will give exercise physiologists financial and career stability.

- A profession that is recognized to educate clients and patients on the necessity for regular exercise to improve their quality of life and prevent the debilitating diseases caused by sedentary living.
- A profession guided by ethical thinking members who understand the need to support and empower the ASEP organization.

Final Thoughts

As Shirley Steele and Vera Harmon (21) said in their book, *Values Clarification in Nursing*, "There comes a time when it is necessary to question, to argue, to challenge." Thus, it is not just okay, it is imperative that exercise physiologists' question, argue, and challenge the present-day academic conditions.

Board Certified Exercise Physiologists can work in hospitals, rehabilitation centers, out-patient clinics, community, corporate, commercial, and university fitness and wellness centers, nursing homes, and senior citizens centers. But, what really is important is that many ASEP members can and do work as healthcare entrepreneurs. This means they are taking responsibility as "Exercise Physiology Entrepreneurs" to help ensure their financial future and access to clients and patients. To better understand the transition process, the following book, *The Business of Exercise Physiology* (22), was written to clarify the specific steps.

Are you willing to pay the price for your personal and professional success as well as the growth of exercise physiology? If you are willing, being successful means taking the time to support the ASEP organization while learning specific business skills. With a daring attitude and action, tenacity and commitment, and sheer perseverance, you will become everything you dreamed to be when you and your parents talked about why you should go to college.

Remember, the dare to be different by thinking about exercise physiology and private practice in the same breath takes guts. While it will not be the career path for every exercise physiologist, it will be a very important alternative to a larger tuition debt. That is why the risk, stress, and responsibility of starting your own healthcare business make sense. So, if you are even slightly thinking about it, take a look at the following questions that need answers, such as:

1. How do I learn the business skills needed to start my own business?
2. Should I start a solo practice or a business with a partner?
3. What about the location?
4. How large should the business space be?
5. What is a business plan?
6. How do I write a business plan?
7. What will be the name of the business?
8. What kind of equipment, new or old, should I buy?
9. How will I market the business to local healthcare practitioners?
10. How will the community learn of the clinic?
11. How many employees should I hire?

Regardless of the pressure to be like everyone else, unhappiness and frustration happen when we reject who we are. The secret to our success as entrepreneurs is to have the courage to acknowledge that we are different. So, in a nutshell, dare to be different. Do not be afraid of your friends, professors, or others and what they may say or think. Change your thinking and you will move beyond the limits placed on exercise physiologists. There simply isn't another way at this time to get what you want and need after college to financially make it. Thus, taking responsibility is the true measure of your instinct for success.

Remember, it is better to be courageous than to give up on what we can become, and, in fact, it is the ultimate measure of each of us. In the end, the destiny of academic exercise physiologists lies in serving their students and in their commitment to supporting ASEP and its caring mindset and ways to manage change by respect and trust. To not acknowledge this thinking is a coward's escape from the work that must be done to stop the educational waste of our non-accredited academic programs going nowhere.

References

1 University of Evansville. (2014). Exercise and Sport Science. Programs. (Online). www.evansville.edu/majors/exss/programs.cfm.
2 Colorado State University. (2015). College of Health and Human Sciences. Sports Medicine. (Online). www.hes.chhs.colostate.edu/students/undergraduate/careers.aspx.
3 Boone, T. (2011). Making the Most of Change. Exercise Physiologists Wordpress. (Online). http://exercisephysiologists.wordpress.com/.
4 Jefferson College of Health Sciences. (2015). Health and Exercise Science. (Online). www.jchs.edu/degree/bachelor-science-health-exercise-science.
5 University of Connecticut. (2014). Exercise Science. Department of Kinesiology. University of Connecticut. (Online). http://ekin.education.uconn.edu.
6 American Society of Exercise Physiologists. (2014). Board Certified Exercise Physiologists. (Online). www.asep.org/?q=services/EPCexam.
7 Greener Grass! (2014). Exercise Physiologists: The 21st century healthcare profession. (Online). http://exercisephysiologists.wordpress.com/page/2/.
8 American Society of Exercise Physiologists. (2016). ASEP Accreditation Manual. (Online). www.asep.org/?q=services/accreditation.
9 Boone, T. (2014). *Introduction to Exercise Physiology*. Burlington, MA: Jones and Bartlett Learning.
10 Sugarman, D. A., & Freeman, L. (1970). *The Search for Serenity: Understanding and overcoming anxiety*. New York: MacMillan Company.
11 Boone, T. (2010). *Integrating Spirituality and Exercise Physiology: Toward a new understanding of health*. Lewiston, NY: The Edwin Mellen Press.
12 Koenig, H. G. (2004). Religion, Spirituality, and Medicine: Research findings and implications for clinical practice. *Southern Medical Journal*, 97: 1194–1200.
13 Ghosh, A. K. (2003). The Role of Religion/Spirituality in the Medical Curriculum. *Minnesota Medicine*, 86: 5.
14 West Virginia University. (2016). School of Medicine: Exercise physiology. (Online). http://medicine.hsc.wvu.edu/ep/education/.

15 Fruscione, J. (2014). When a College Contracts 'Adjunctivitis,' It's the Students Who Lose. PBSNewshour. (Online). www.pbs.org/newshour/making-sense/when-a-college-contracts-adjunctivitis-its-the-students-who-lose/.
16 Kendzoir, S. (2014). What Is the Point of Academic Publishing? (Online). https://chroniclevitae.com/news/291-what-s-the-point-of-academic-publishing.
17 Millman, D. (2013). Brandonsneed. (Online). http://brandonsneed.com/quote-imagination-and-what-you-deserve/.
18 Bureau of Labor Statistics. (2018). U.S. Department of Labor, Occupational Outlook Handbook, Job Outlook, Exercise Physiologists. April 13, 2018. (Online). www.bls.gov/ooh/healthcare/exercise-physiologists.htm#tab-6.
19 Boone, T. (2016). *ASEP's Exercise Medicine Text for Exercise Physiologists*. Beijing, China: Bentham Science Publishing.
20 Wattles, M. (2001). The Exercise Physiology Time Bomb: A wakeup call for exercise physiology professors. *Professionalization of Exercise Physiology-online*, 4: 2.
21 Steele, S. M., & Harmon, V. M. (1979). *Values Clarification in Nursing*. New York: Appleton-Century-Crofts.
22 Boone, T. (2012). *The Business of Exercise Physiology*. Lewiston, NY: The Edwin Mellen Press.

9

OUR DESTINY IS EXERCISE MEDICINE

> Exercise medicine has wide-ranging health benefits, particularly from the prevention point of view. Whether it is type 2 diabetes or some forms of cancer, there is enhanced function with age. There is also very strong research to support the prescription of exercise as the drug of choice in dealing with cognitive decline.

It is just a matter of time before Board Certified Exercise Physiologists will be acknowledged as *the* healthcare professionals to administer exercise medicine. Clients and patients with non-communicable chronic diseases complain of muscular aches and pain and shortness of breath that are associated with difficulty at work and at home. The practice of exercise medicine is a major part of the ASEP exercise physiology vision with the expectation of helping clients live with less pain and disability. The ASEP Board Certified Exercise Physiologists have the academic training to exercise ethical judgment within their scope of practice. They are healthcare professionals responsible for helping clients and patients incorporate exercise medicine into their daily routines.

> Professionalism is an important component of exercise physiology's contract with society. Without question, there is an ethical need to teach professionalism to the students of exercise physiology.

The Power of a Title

Thinking as an "ASEP Board Certified Exercise Physiologist" can change the person who understands the importance of the title. There is power and comfort in knowing who you are, and other people recognize it. For example, a person may say, "I am a medical doctor" while another may say, "I am a lawyer." Immediately, we begin to treat each person with respect. The same should be true for the "exercise physiologist" title, but first society has to understand what the title means, and the academic work required to be a Board Certified Exercise Physiologist. Without the work of the ASEP organization, why would someone in the public sector value the title?

Despite the work of the ASEP leaders, many academic exercise physiologists are notoriously bad at accepting ASEP and its vision. It is a stumbling block, but it will be resolved as ASEP continues its work to raise current thinking to the Board Certified Exercise Physiologist level and as college teachers assume more responsibility and accountability for their students' well-being. Commitment to generic organizations, faculty credentials, and emphasis on research rather than professionalism are among the primary issues that must be addressed. And yet, professionalism and board certification are critical to earning the respect of the public and eventually in exercise physiologists' becoming self-regulated through licensure.

> **What we must learn is the role of being a professional versus a specialist and we must have a clear vision that can lead us in the right direction.**

A college graduate with an exercise physiology degree is exactly what the degree title means. Hence, individuals with an exercise science or a kinesiology degree cannot refer to themselves as an exercise physiologist any more than they can say I am a physical therapist. Having all exercise physiologists hold the same degree designation will reduce the public confusion that arises when multiple degree titles are talked about. As exercise physiologists become more homogeneous, they will be recognized as the primary exercise medicine practitioners.

The true value of an academic degree lies in the completion of the degree and its link to one's courage to be different in how the degree is used. The truth is exercise physiology majors can make significantly more use of their degree than an exercise science major. They understand the power in the exercise physiology title, the healthcare possibilities, and in particular the scientific benefits of exercise. That is why the ASEP exercise physiologists are spreading the message that they are healthcare professionals while many colleagues are saying very little because they are uncomfortable with challenging the norm, which is a major problem.

> **Board Certified Exercise Physiologists are known for their specialized knowledge. They have a strong professional commitment to develop and improve their knowledge and hands-on skills to practice successfully and to deliver the best care to their clients and patients.**

Exercise physiologists have the theoretical knowledge to practice exercise medicine and, in particular, the ASEP Board Certified Exercise Physiologists understand that exercise improves mood, slows aging, and decreases chronic pain. This point is important, especially since the majority of kids and adolescents in America have what Mandy Oaklander refers to as "exercise-deficit disorder." Hence, given that nearly half of the high school students don't have weekly PE classes, exercise physiologists are prepared to help build up and maintain the students' health and well-being.

Please appreciate that these comments bear witness to more than the usual recommendation "to get some exercise every week" or "you should get 30 minutes of moderate-intensity exercise on most days of the week." The exercise medicine prescription is about systematic testing and teaching clients that increasing physical activity results in physiologic improvements in cardiovascular endurance, muscle strength, endurance, and flexibility, body composition, insulin sensitivity, and lipid levels. Also, the prescription will include a detailed exercise plan that involves teaching behavioral management skills and how to maintain regular exercise. Clients need a more engaging understanding of aerobic functions and oxygen that is transported from the lungs to the tissues during exercise and what happens at the tissue level in addition to how exercise might benefit the brain by improving blood flow, decreasing depression, and improving memory.

The ASEP exercise physiologists have stepped up to the plate with their focus on changing behavior, ethical thinking, academic accreditation, board certification, and standards of professional practice. Their goal is to provide the information to motivate and empower clients and patients to change their lifestyle behaviors by focusing on the cognitive skills and attitudes that prompt a new way to look at the exercise as regenerative medicine. This shift to educate the public sector about the health and fitness issues is necessary to enhance society's understanding of how regular exercise extends life span by as much as five years.

The ASEP leaders believe the Board Certified Exercise Physiologists will play a pivotal role in promoting autonomous practice of exercise physiology, given their increased focus on business skills to secure self-employment. Yes, all of these things are worthy goals to work towards. As Leo F. Buscaglia said, "The person who risks nothing does nothing, has nothing, is nothing, and becomes nothing. He may avoid suffering and sorrow, but he simply cannot learn and feel and change and grow and love and live."

A New Healthcare Profession

The ASEP effort to create a new healthcare profession is exciting because it will bring great joy to thousands of exercise physiologists in decades to come. They will get the big picture, and they will follow through with the ASEP vision and goals. As ASEP members, they will appreciate that success is built on focusing their energy on the professionalization of exercise physiology. They will no longer fall victim to the failed rhetoric of yesterday's thinking, which is consistent with the thoughts of the author Harry A. Overstreet who observed that, "The immature mind hops from one thing to another; the mature mind seeks to follow through."

> At times it seems that academic exercise physiologists are simply too scared to think differently. And yet, it is important to put the past behind us and move on. Cut ties from physical education and move on! When all else fails, give yourself permission to be different and establish your own boundaries of what is important.

The exercise specialist thinking of years ago and the personal trainer thinking of today is wrong for exercise physiologists. Such thinking will keep exercise physiologists from achieving their destiny. Instead, they must stop looking back, get rid of the distractions, and give full attention to thinking about their future in the profession of exercise physiology.

Their thinking is not complicated or wrong. It is their decision to stop giving up who they are because others say it has always been this way. Robert Frost said it best, "Two roads diverged in a wood, and I ... I took the one less traveled by, and that has made all the difference."

As more academic exercise physiologists take the less traveled ASEP path, it will make a difference in the lives of their students. Also, while research is fun to do, uplifting, and important, it cannot substitute for the necessary breadth and depth in educational preparation to professionalize exercise physiology. The 21st century ASEP leaders provide unprecedented opportunities to impact positively the needs of all exercise physiologists. They are interested in dealing with the unforeseen challenges to students and promoting the professionalization process, not publishing more papers.

The profession needs the support of exercise physiologists with the imagination and desire to help the ASEP leaders in the advancement, development, teaching, and practice of exercise physiology. Why not ask yourself the following questions and compare your responses:

1. ***Why is it important for exercise physiologists to join ASEP?*** *Answer:* According to Soren Kierkegaard, it is as simple as, "To dare is to lose one's footing momentarily. To not dare is to lose oneself."
2. ***What are exercise physiologists going to miss by not joining ASEP?*** *Answer:* According to W. E. B. Du Bois, "The most important thing to remember is this: to be ready at any moment to give up what you are for what you might become."
3. ***Why do academic exercise physiologists tell the ASEP leaders they are supporting the short end of the stick?*** *Answer:* According to Tim Ferriss, here is what the ASEP leadership has learned. "Think big and don't listen to people who tell you it can't be done. Life's too short to think small."

4. ***What would happen to exercise physiology if the process of change took place sooner than later?*** *Answer:* H. Jackson Brown says, "Twenty years from now you will be more disappointed by the things that you didn't do than by the ones you did do, so throw off the bowlines, sail away from safe harbor, and catch the trade winds in your sails. Explore, dream, discover."

Creative and new ideas must exist if change is to take place. That is why ASEP is important to exercise physiology, especially since it has opened the door to new thinking and the passion to break out of the old exercise science mentality. That way the impossible is possible with the ASEP organization.

ASEP is interested in promoting cohesion and marketing exercise physiologists, especially the Board Certified Exercise Physiologists. The academic accreditation document is comprehensive, which is the case for Board Certification. Members of the Board of Directors (BOD) are confident that the ASEP strategic planning is aligned with the master plan of other healthcare organizations. The BOD is not lukewarm in its conviction. It is confident that ASEP is doing what the students need to be successful after graduation. Hence, it is a matter of time that all exercise physiologists will get the message; a profession-specific organization is prerequisite to career success of all exercise physiologists.

The icing on the cake is that the members of ASEP think in terms of "I can" versus "I can't." Their attitude of "possibilities" and their faith are vital to the active process of change and being successful. One person in particular with the conviction that all is well with ASEP is Dr. Frank Wyatt. He is a professor of exercise physiology who teaches at Midwestern State University in Wichita Falls, TX. His faith in ASEP is built up from belief and trust that a profession-specific organization fulfills the social and moral support to help exercise physiologists perform their ethical duties and professional roles in the practice of exercise physiology.

Dr. Wyatt did what was necessary to get both the undergraduate exercise physiology degree and the graduate exercise physiology degree accredited by ASEP. Prior to the graduation of his senior students, they sit for the ASEP Board Certification exam to earn the professional title, Board Certified Exercise Physiologist. Please appreciate that none of what Dr. Wyatt has done is naive or foolish. On the contrary, it is the result of a powerful desire to do what is right and the determination to act in light of his beliefs. He is a positive role model for academic exercise physiologists to emulate.

It is a day to be remembered and talked about when a professional stands up and says, "Enough with status quo!" When it happens, that person is a thinker who believes that, "If you think you can accomplish great things as a member of ASEP, you are right." As we all know, life is hard. Attitude is everything. The power of one's mind to accomplish their goals is the driving force behind success. Few people accomplish much in life with the attitude, "It can't be done." Conversely, when they say, "It can be done"—change is possible. And that's it, as Shane Paulson, the CEO of ASEP says, "All it takes is the right attitude."

Interestingly, what will happen with the changed thinking is that the older non-changed academic exercise physiologists will eventually retire. It is the young exercise physiologists with the ASEP mindset who are more likely to encourage the department chair and the administration to change the degree title and the curriculum to the ASEP exercise physiology perspective. As that happens, the students' lives will improve both in and out of the academic setting. The idea of getting a generic degree without the possibility of securing a credible job will gradually disappear.

Remember if ASEP exercise physiologists believe they can change exercise physiology from a research discipline to a healthcare profession, they can, and it will be done! That is the power of understanding that, "*We are what we think*." Hence, since the ASEP exercise physiologists believe they are more than a fitness instructor or a trainer, they must remove themselves from the popular rhetoric of sports medicine and exercise science. The old ways and ideas handed down from the old academy must be discarded for what they are—"Yesterday's thinking."

There is a better and a more meaningful way. That way is ASEP and its vision of exercise physiology as a healthcare profession with the shared scientific education, ethical standards, and unique professional hands-on laboratory skills to prescribe exercise medicine to clients and patients of all ages.

Exercise Medicine

Yesterday, a friend said: "I wish I had a pill that would keep me healthy." He was not talking about a drug such as atenolol for high blood pressure or diabetes. As our conversation continued, it was clear that he wanted a pill that would produce physiologic changes similar to what takes place when a person engages in regular exercise. He wanted what is known as an "exercise pill." After a deep breath I looked him in the eyes and said, "Actually, researchers have been working on developing a drug that causes the body to respond as though it had just completed an exercise session" (1–3).

His comment was, "Really, where can I get some?" I said, "Presently, the research has been done only with mice. Of course, all you need to do is to start a walking program 3 $d \cdot wk^{-1}$." He said, "No way, I want a pill. I don't want to exercise." It was clear that he was not interested in exercising. Also, he was not interested in a physiologic evaluation prior to starting an exercise medicine program. His mind was made up. He wanted to be healthy and strong without exercising. His response did not come as a surprise since most people are not interested in exercising. Everybody knows that it is not easy to start an exercise program much less stay with it. It is even a challenge to get a client to get involved in a relaxation program once or twice a week to reduce stress.

Because exercise physiologists have the scientific education to understand and promote the physiological benefits of exercise training to increase athletic performance, they also understand the specificity associated with regular exercise as an effective way to decrease the risk of cardiovascular disease and a host of other diseases and disabilities. This is especially true for ASEP Board Certified Exercise Physiologists. However, while it is popular for researchers to identify an actual "exercise pill" (i.e., a drug) that may become the equivalent of exercising, the ASEP position is that the healthcare emphasis should be exercise medicine. More often than not researchers are finding that exercise leads to better outcomes than drugs. In fact, it is amazing to see sick patients engaged in regular exercise experience improvements in anxiety, mood, depression, and energy levels.

The ASEP Board Certified Exercise Physiologists are not interested in prescribing an exercise pill, but rather in prescribing exercise medicine (as though it is a drug). There is a big difference in the two points of view. Although the idea of an exercise pill (drug) is very appealing to men and women of all ages, it raises many questions:

1. Is the exercise pill the answer to the many hours that adults spend in sedentary behavior?
2. Will the pill correct society's obesity, hypertension, and depression to mention three of the several major causes of death and disability in the United States and worldwide?
3. If the exercise pill reduces risk factors that threatening human health, how long will it work, and is it age- or gender-specific?
4. How much will the pill cost, and will it be covered by insurance?
5. Will the exercise pill benefit both sexes and all ages similarly or differently and for how long will the effects last?
6. Will the exercise pill require some exercise and, if so, how much exercise is sufficient to improve and/or maintain the musculoskeletal system versus the cardiorespiratory system?
7. Will the exercise pill result in physiological adaptations as does regular exercise, such as the decrease in exercise double product, myocardial oxygen consumption, and relative cardiac efficiency?
8. Will the exercise pill do everything that exercise does for the mind, particularly the improvement in well-being?
9. Will the exercise pill control the percentage of body fat in children, adolescents, and adults in the way or differently?
10. Will the exercise pill promote fun, enjoyment, and well-being among friends and family?
11. Will the cost of the exercise pill be intolerable and/or have potential toxicities?
12. Is it wise to consume an exercise pill that may alter a person's circadian rhythms, internal biological clocks, and energy expenditure?
13. Does the dream of effortless fitness from large doses of an exercise drug versus an individualized exercise medicine prescription make sense (except for individuals who can't exercise or otherwise limited in their ability to so)?
14. Is it likely that an exercise pill will ever duplicate the multiplicity of physiologic, respiratory, and metabolic responses that occur with exercise medicine,

not to mention the power of regular exercise to promote mental and emotional health and well-being?

Since the federal government (4) issued its first national exercise guidelines in 2008, there is the general acceptance that an increase in physical activity protects against chronic diseases (such as coronary artery disease, hypertension, and some forms of cancer) and disabilities. Interestingly, even though the medical community understands the importance of regular exercise, why is it that only approximately 40% of the medical doctors talk to their patients about exercise?

It appears that the majority of the medical doctors would rather tell their patients about the benefits of a particular drug to prevent a heart attack or a stroke, to enable ambulation, improve circulation, and promote relaxation. After all, it is easier to prescribe a pill or a combination of different pills than to take the time to talk with patients about their unhealthy lifestyle behaviors and the specifics of an exercise prescription.

If the conversation between the physician and the patient is not about surgery to reduce body fat, it is about the exercise pill to burn fat. Why? The answer is because the idea of an exercise pill is gaining popularity as the means to improving the nation's health problems. If such a pill should exist for human beings, it is reasonable to conclude that it would replace exercise (given that a very small percent of Americans take time to exercise in the first place). It would be the answer to our health problems or at least society would think that is the case!

> With so many people unwilling to make a change in their sedentary lifestyle, the "exercise pill" could be just what the doctor ordered.

If everyone would purchase "compound 14" (a molecule created by scientists at the University of Southampton in Great Britain) (6) to decrease percent body fat, there would be no body fat disease-oriented problems. Perhaps that would be the outcome. No one really knows, however. Imagine the potential benefits of a molecule that mimics exercise by setting off a chemical reaction tricking cells into thinking they have run low on energy causing them to increase metabolism and uptake of glucose that improves glucose tolerance and promotes weight loss (i.e., at least as determined in obese mice). Of course, the reality is that before the "exercise pill" becomes available to the public sector, the long-term effects on human volunteers must be determined.

I asked my brother, "What makes more sense Ed, regular exercise or taking an exercise pill?" He said, "Well, I admit that I have never exercised much and, frankly, I'm not that interested in exercising. If there is a magic exercise pill that I can take every day or every other day, I want it." Then I said,

"To my understanding there will not be such a pill for the general public anytime soon. So, if you want to avoid sarcopenia (i.e., the wasting of your muscles) with aging and/or the predisposition to chronic diseases (myocardial infarction and stroke, in particular) associated with your sedentary lifestyle, you will need to engage in a regular exercise program. Perhaps, there will be an exercise pill in the future that will be available like other drugs, but not now."

> Understandably, it makes sense that some disease conditions are not corrected by exercise, thus requiring the use of different medications. But, just because the majority of society is not willing to engage in regular exercise to deal with chronic diseases and/or disabilities, is it logical or ethical to promote an "exercise pill" as a substitute for lack of discipline in caring for one's health?

In *Treads in Pharmacological Sciences*, Ismail Laher of the Department of Pharmacology and Therapeutics at University of British Columbia in Vancouver and Shunchang Li (7) of Beijing Sport University said that with an increased understanding of how exercise influences molecular pathways, the development of an exercise pill is feasible for some of the benefits. The statement is a hopeful benefit of positive changes in structure and function to help avoid or minimize certain diseases and/or disabilities.

Narkar and colleagues (8) studied AICAR in mice for 4 weeks and reported that it induced changes in metabolic genes and enhanced running endurance by 44%. They concluded that AICAR enhanced the training adaptation by activating AMP-activated protein kinase (AMPK), which stimulates glucose uptake by the skeletal muscle cells. Then, AMPK interacts with another protein (PGC–1x) that results in the improvement of oxidative metabolism, mitochondrial biogenesis, fiber-type transformation in skeletal muscles, and ATP production. The lead researcher, Ronald Evans of the Salk Institute said, "It's tricking the muscle into 'believing' it's been exercised daily," and "… it proves you can have a pharmacologic equivalent to exercise."

Another pharmacologic equivalent is known as GW501516 (also known on the black market as Endurobol), which was created by Ligand Pharmaceuticals and GlaxoSmithKline in the 1990s as a drug for metabolic and cardiovascular diseases (9). It was abandoned in 2007 because animal testing showed that it caused cancer to develop in numerous organs (such as the liver, bladder, stomach, skin, thyroid, tongue, testes, ovaries, and womb). When the drug was given in high doses to mice, their physical performance dramatically improved. Athletes understand what this means, and they are abusing the drug as a doping agent (10). The World Anti-Doping Agency (WADA) developed a test for GW501516 and other related chemicals and added them to the prohibited list in 2009. WADA has issued additional warnings to athletes that GW501516 is not safe.

According to Laher and Li (7), the exercise pill "… cannot act as a substitute for all the benefits of physical activity." They also said that, "It is unrealistic to expect that exercise pills will fully be able to substitute for physical exercise …." Hence, it looks like my brother will have to bite the bullet and put on his walking shoes, that is, if he interested in counteracting the consequences of physical inactivity that include a decrease in body's sensitivity to insulin, an increase in the storage of body fat, and a confirmed scientific relationship between a decrease in quality of health and longevity. Also, it is important to point out that an exercise pill is not likely to have a positive link to endorphins that come from exercising.

Given the limitations of an exercise pill, is my brother setting himself up to fail? Now that we know that regular exercise is the equivalent of medicine, why shouldn't he simply embrace exercise medicine? The short answer is that some people simply are not interested in exercising, but they may enjoy physical work around the house (which is what my brother does). He is more interested in keeping the yard cut and all the other things that go into maintaining a nice home.

In general, however, it is common knowledge that individuals of all ages are interested in a quick fix for their problems. Regardless of age and gender, the majority of Americans and individuals worldwide are not presently interested in exercise medicine, although they should be to realize the mind and body benefits of regular exercise. The idea of waiting for an exercise pill to solve society's health problems is not the right answer to acknowledging that we, the people, must do our part to be healthy.

While an exercise pill is appealing for people who can't exercise due to paralysis or other reasons, the point is that exercise medicine is already self-evident. This is a major awakening to the healthcare community and, in particular, the profession of exercise physiology from an entrepreneurial perspective. Although ASEP is a young organization, the leaders created the first-ever professional infrastructure to promote professionalism and entrepreneurship in exercise physiology (11–13). They understand that exercise is the magic exercise medicine every person needs to empower the mind, to strengthen the skeletal system, and to prevent coronary heart disease and some cancers. ASEP Board Certified Exercise Physiologists are in a great position to implement a safe exercise medicine prescription for children and adults of all ages.

The couch potato must stop looking for the exercise pill in the mail. The researchers must think long and hard about creating such a pill for the sedentary population. Either it is a dream or a misdirected way of thinking, similar to the cheating and doping that is popular but unethical in athletics (14). For certain it is the wrong thinking to help with the life-changing lifestyle decisions that are necessary to help prevent chronic diseases and/or disabilities. The idea that we need a pill, so we can continue our poor lifestyle habits of physical inactivity, watching too much TV, failing to exercise regularly, consuming too many calories, and living with too much stress and tension, and not addressing our anxiety is misguided thinking.

> It sounds too good to be true and, perhaps, it is. Everyone is looking for an exercise pill.

Is it cruel and hurtful to categorize physically inactive Americans as lazy or weak-willed? I'm not sure. Please appreciate that it is not my intent to do so. But, the bottom line is this: Life is about making choices. Either we can decide to exercise, or we can hasten our death by living a sedentary lifestyle. The fact that many adults are interested in an exercise pill means that the pharmaceutical industry continues to win the battle of financial profits over common sense living.

Even now we look for a pill when we have a headache during and/or after work while failing to do anything positive about the stress and anxiety with colleagues. Thus, it seems that we need an exercise pill for our failure to monitor stress, to exercise our heart and lungs to be healthy, and to lift weights to keep our muscles strong and flexible. Otherwise, without the exercise pill we will have to either experience the act of exercising and benefits thereof or grow old and sick prematurely.

It is interesting that hardly anyone disagrees with taking an exercise pill to mimic the effects of going to the gym. Perhaps it is obvious that we need something to avoid premature death, given that we fail to live a healthy lifestyle? While we realize psychologically what we are doing, deep down we accept the idea of popping a pill because it has become part of our culture and who we are as human beings. No doubt similar thinking goes into using sports supplements and drugs to increase the athletes' chance of winning. It is easier to cheat to win than to put in the work to increase the likelihood of winning (14). The magic "athletic pill" to win is the equivalent of the magic "exercise pill" to obtain fitness without working for it.

A healthier life is possible for most individuals, and exercise medicine is the key to a healthier mind and body. Those who exercise are likely to break a sweat, experience excitement, and understand being bored at times. That is life. It is about doing what has to be done to get good grades in college, to keep a job, to connect with that special person, to be successful in sports, and to be mentally and physically healthy. The benefits of exercise medicine come with a price and that is the willingness to exercise.

Exercise enhances who we are and even how we influence others while also living a healthier lifestyle. The obvious question is, "Why the lack of interest in exercise?" One answer is rather common: "I didn't enjoy PE or sports in high school. I am not athletic and, frankly, I would rather watch TV or read a book." Additional reasons include feeling less than competent or, perhaps, a physical limitation renders a person awkward or unable to exercise. Obviously, life isn't fair in dozens of ways. But, because it is so precious we should think positive and do what is necessary to keep going. More often than not, this means doing things outside of our comfort zone. Then, after weeks, months, or years walking and/or jogging, we may learn to appreciate that regular exercise is as vital to a healthy life as brushing our teeth.

Exercise medicine contributes to the primary and secondary prevention of non-communicable diseases. Similarly, from a somewhat different perspective, who among us would want to try living a wonderful life without any muscular strength, endurance, or flexibility? Each is required to perform many of the activities of daily living, which is also true for the body's ability to transport and use oxygen during life's daily activities. Each is acquired as a positive outcome of an individualized exercise medicine prescription.

A person who is thinking about starting an exercise training program should understand that even a modest improvement in daily physical activities (such as walking, jogging, or riding a bicycle) can yield tangible benefits in well-being and longevity. Also, while it is apparent that an exercise pill is not likely to produce acute and chronic adaptations in the body as does regular exercise, the focus on the partial effects of regular exercise (such as increasing metabolism) is a limited view of what must be achieved, maintained, and enhanced to be healthy.

When compared to the exercise pill, a person who engages in regular exercise will demonstrate a lower resting and exercise heart rate with a higher stroke volume, which means the heart needs less oxygen to pump the required blood volume (i.e., cardiac output) to the peripheral tissues. Also, aside from the exercise training effect of a greater oxygen extraction by the muscles, regular exercise increases the size (hypertrophy), strength, and endurance of the muscular system (11).

In addition, regular exercise helps to decrease many of the commonly prescribed medications such as statins and anti-platelet drugs. Regular exercise increases joint flexibility while taking an exercise pill is not likely to produce an increase in range of joint motion. It will not increase mental health, self-esteem, cognitive ability, and cardiorespiratory function and yet, exercise medicine can do those things and more (such as):

- Lower the risk of early death
- Lower the risk of coronary heart disease
- Lower the risk of stroke
- Lower the risk of hypertension
- Lower the risk of adverse blood lipid profile
- Lower the risk of type 2 diabetes
- Lower the risk of metabolic syndrome
- Lower the risk of hip fracture
- Lower the frequency of falls
- Lower the risk of lung cancer
- Lower the risk of colon cancer
- Lower the risk of breast cancer
- Prevent weight gain
- Decrease abdominal obesity
- Decrease the symptoms of depression
- Increase cognitive function
- Increase sleep quality
- Improve the cardiovascular and metabolic health biomarkers

> The change in the relationship between stroke volume and heart rate under the influence of exercise medicine is a positive hemodynamic adaptation that decreases the overall work of the heart.

The Vascular Perspective

Exercise is the equivalent of a drug that helps to normalize the cardiovascular system. That is why physical activity and regular exercise are known by the popular expression: Exercise Is Medicine. However, from the ASEP perspective, the correct expression is Exercise Medicine (15). A person who exercises has a higher exercise capacity than someone who does not exercise, which correlates with a larger, individualized dose of exercise medicine that decreases mortality from coronary disease and/or other chronic diseases (16).

While the benefits of exercise medicine include structural and physiological changes that diminish the risk of different diseases, there are also beneficial effects of exercise on the vascular cells. The biology of the endothelial cells reveals a variety of health-related functions, particularly the impact of exercise medicine on restoring a healthy endothelial phenotype.

The effect of exercise medicine on muscle tissue that contracts to produce movement is linked to vasodilation and the enhanced blood flow throughout the contracting muscle tissues. The result is an increase in the hemodynamic forces (i.e., shear stress and cyclic strain) and/or circulating factors that are released from the adipose tissue and skeletal muscle that are believed to initiate endothelial adaptations in the arteries that supply the skeletal muscles and nonworking tissues (17).

There is also scientific evidence that the exercise medicine produces adaptations in the healthy as well as in the unhealthy individuals (11). This means exercise medicine should be prescribed to everyone, regardless of age, sex, healthy, or unhealthy. Individuals with preexisting cardiovascular risk factors benefit from regular exercise training just as non-diseased individuals do.

Exercise medicine is statistically associated with a decrease in strokes (e.g., cerebrovascular events) by decreasing the arterial stiffness and the risk of carotid artery plaque, the likelihood of a rupture, and emboli. Hence, exercise medicine is anti-atherogenic by decreasing a person's oxidative stress through the up-regulation of the antioxidant enzyme, superoxide dismutase.

There are also exercise medicine-induced improvements in functional and cognitive outcomes due to the positive changes in vasodilator action and cerebral circulation in specific regions of the brain. Exercise medicine increases cardiac output (i.e., the volume of blood ejected from each ventricle per minute) that results in an increased blood flow across the endothelium, which increases a shear stress stimulus that increases the production and release of nitric oxide (NO) by the endothelium to dilate the vessels (18).

Exercise medicine also triggers improvements in cardiorespiratory fitness, efficiency, and blood pressure. Specifically, with respect to the lungs, both at rest and during exercise, ventilation is improved with a larger tidal volume and a lower frequency of breaths per minute. Similarly, the improved left ventricle that pumps a larger stroke volume to the peripheral tissues does so while the heart beats less frequently per minute (heart rate). Exercise medicine improves the extraction of oxygen (i.e., a-vO_2 difference) by the skeletal muscles as well as the removal of carbon dioxide from the tissues. The reduced fasting blood glucose and the increased insulin sensitivity also help to protect against the non-active lifestyle related diseases (19).

> The change in the relationship between stroke volume and heart rate under the influence of exercise medicine is a positive hemodynamic adaptation that decreases the overall work of the heart.

While physical inactivity is a major risk factor that contributes to chronic diseases (such as high blood pressure, heart disease, and type 2 diabetes mellitus), exercise medicine produces myocardial and skeletal muscle adaptations and remodeling. These changes set the stage for the increase in substrate delivery and utilization, mitochondrial density and respiration, intrinsic oxidative capacity, contractile function, and resistance to fatigue. Exercise medicine also increases skeletal muscle glucose uptake through an insulin-dependent pathway.

Both aerobic training and resistance training are effective in decreasing insulin resistance in obesity and metabolic syndrome and improving glycemic control in type 2 diabetes mellitus (19). Muscle hypertrophy and neurological adaptations represent two additional important changes that increase muscle function. The latter is the result of the collective improvements in motor unit activation, firing frequency, and synchrony of high-intensity motor units. This is true for the increase in athletic performance as well as the improvement in health-related musculoskeletal function.

Physiology of Exercise Medicine

Professionalism is steadily growing in most healthcare professions. As exercise medicine becomes popular with the public sector, society will want to be led by credible healthcare professionals. The idea of just any person interested in fitness applying the scientific principles of exercise physiology is scary. In fact, it is safe to say that just because an individual seems to be in good shape does not mean he or she knows anything about the physiology of the musculoskeletal system or the psychophysiology of exercise training.

Recently, I was engaged in a brief conversation with an emerging leader in the personal training field. We talked about oxygen consumption, fitness, and training.

Here is what he had to say about oxygen consumption. "Consuming oxygen is like using gas in a car. The faster you go the more oxygen you need." I said, "Yes, but not all cars are built to get 25 miles per gallon or drive fast." Then, I said, "If something fails to work, can you take the motor apart, meaning can you identify the musculoskeletal and physiological problem(s)? By the way, do you know the origin and insertion of the muscles that flex the shoulder joint and the nerves to each?" He named two of the five muscles. He did not know the nerves to the shoulder flexors. Then, I asked, "Is it a requirement to drive fast to keep the car running good?" He said, "Yes, that is why my clients are pushed to go all out in their exercise sessions with me." I said, "Isn't it important to consider the physical condition of the client?" He said, "Why, if they want to get fit, then they need to do what I tell them to do."

As an exercise physiologist, I think it is important to know how to calculate a client's oxygen consumption (VO_2), cardiac output (Q), and tissue extraction (a-vO_2 diff). I asked the personal trainer if he was aware of regression equations that he could use to estimate his client's VO_2 while exercising. He said, "I don't need to know anything about VO_2 and I don't need to calculate it." I said, "Well, it is important to know because it is the physiological product of cardiac output and arteriovenous oxygen difference (i.e., a-vO_2 diff)."

He looked at me for about a minute without saying anything. His expression was one of confusion. After a few breaths and looking elsewhere he turned to me and said, "I know the heart pumps blood to the body, but what is the 'difference' thing?" I told him, "It is the difference between the oxygen in the arterial blood and the venous blood and how much oxygen is consumed by the muscles at rest and during exercise."

Then, I said, "At rest an average VO_2 for a 70 kg (i.e., 154 lb) person is ~250 $mL \cdot min^{-1}$ or 0.25 $L \cdot min^{-1}$. It is (on average) the product of a cardiac output of 5 $L \cdot min^{-1}$ times a tissue extraction (a-vO_2 diff) of 50 mL of $O_2 \cdot L^{-1}$ of blood." I looked at the trainer and ask him the question, "Do you understand?" He said, "No, I don't know what you are talking about! Do I actually need to know that?" I said, "Yes, you need to know that and much more! For example, you need to know that ventilation (V_E) increases with the increase in the intensity of exercise, and that it is the product of tidal volume (T_V) and frequency of breaths (Fb). You need to know the difference between V_E and alveolar ventilation (V_A), and the importance of a large T_V versus Fb."

This idea is similar to the efficiency of cardiac output, especially since it should be produced primarily by stroke volume (SV) rather than by heart rate (HR). The higher the SV for a steady-state exercise Q the lower the HR. This means the heart (i.e., myocardium) is more efficient in its delivery of oxygen to the peripheral skeletal muscle tissues. This point is supported by the double product equation (DP), which is an excellent estimate of the work of the heart (i.e., DP = HR x SBP x 0.01).

As an example of the importance of DP and what it reveals, assume that SBP is unchanged at the same submaximal steady-state exercise after training while the client's HR is lower. This means DP is lower and the heart is not working as hard as it did before training. The decreased work of the heart means that it requires less oxygen. This is a positive physiologic training response since myocardial oxygen consumption (MVO_2) is correlated with the subject's DP (19). By lowering DP, the heart's need for oxygen is decreased (which can be estimated by the formula: MVO_2 = 0.14(DP) – 6.3). Similarly, if a client's T_V is high either at rest or during exercise, then, the lower the Fb for a given V_E. Hence, in both instances the lungs and the heart are more efficient in bringing in oxygen and transporting it to the skeletal muscles.

After looking at the trainer, it occurred to me I was talking to myself. With the next breath I asked the trainer, "Do you understand the relationship of the size of the heart to a person's body size." He looked at me as though I had lost my mind. He said, "Why is there a relationship between a person's body size and the heart?" I said, "There is a relationship. The average heart weighs about 306 g in a 70 kg person." He asked, "How do you know that?" I said, "The following equations approximate the weight of an untrained person's heart. For example, the equation HW = (2.54 kgBW) + 128 can be used for men, and the equation HW = (2.10 x kgBW) + 126 can used to estimate the weight of a woman's heart" (11).

I said, "Notice the word 'untrained' because the equation is not likely to apply with the same relative accuracy to well-trained athletes." He just stared at me! Then, I said, "The reason is that regular aerobic exercise increases the size of the heart, particularly the ventricles. In the aerobic athlete, the large left ventricle is a positive adaptation to the large venous return, which is referred to as the large left ventricular end-diastolic volume that ultimately increases stroke volume when the ventricle contracts. This left ventricular adaptation allows for a more efficient cardiac output (i.e., the volume of blood and oxygen in it that is ejected to the peripheral tissues throughout the body). With the increase in the subject's oxygen at the muscle tissue level, more energy in the form of adenosine triphosphate (ATP, the energy currency of life) is generated by the electron transport system (ETS) within the mitochondria of the muscle cells."

The trainer said, "Honestly, do I need to know what you are saying to lead my clients through an exercise session?" I said, "No, not really but it would be best if you did know the **physiology of exercise medicine** for safety and ethical reasons." He said, "Okay, then, tell me more!" I said, "Sure, but keep in mind that I am not even touching the tip of the physiology of exercise medicine iceberg. The content of exercise physiology and all the academic courses that define an ASEP accredited exercise physiology degree is comprehensive. That is why the exercise physiology students study the cardiorespiratory system, functional anatomy, biomechanics, sports nutrition, electrocardiography, research and statistics, and dozens of metabolic laboratory assessment techniques."

I said to the trainer,

> "ASEP defines an exercise physiologist as someone who has a college degree in exercise physiology or who has passed the ASEP Board Certification exam. It is incorrect and, in fact, unethical for a person with a degree in exercise science or kinesiology or one of a dozen other degree programs to refer to themselves as an exercise physiologist. Unfortunately, though, too many people with an art

degree or an accounting degree think that all they need to do is get a personal trainer certification and, then, they can start their own fitness and healthcare business. Imagine the chaos that would come from a host of other professions in which a person would simply get a weekend warrior pass to engage a client in the use of drugs, update an expensive business computer, or perform any function that requires a specialized and engaging education."

After a few minutes, the trainer took a deep breath and said, "Will you take a moment to explain the importance of knowing the MVO_2 equation you mentioned earlier?" I said, "Do you recall that DP is the product of HR and SBP? If one or both is increased at rest or during exercise, the work of the heart is increased. This means that the heart needs more oxygen. That is not a problem as long as the heart can get the oxygen it needs. Of course, the issue is whether the coronary arteries can supply the heart with an increase in blood flow to provide the oxygen it needs to do the work that is required of it."

Then I said,

"Let us assume that a client I have been working with complains of chest pain earlier in the day before his appointment with me. The fact that I understand the chest pain might be a precursor to a heart attack (i.e., myocardial infarction) is important. Let us assume that his normal resting HR and SBP are 70 beats·min^{-1} and 120 mmHg, respectively, with a calculated DP of 84. But, today, his resting HR and SBP are 140 beats·min^{-1} and 180 mmHg, respectively, then his DP is 252 or 3 times higher than it should be. Once again, if he had good blood flow to the heart, there shouldn't be a problem. However, until his resting DP returns to normal resting values, it is not advisable for him to exercise. In this instance, I would recommend that he calls his family doctor and explain what is going on."

Here, we can estimate how much oxygen is needed at the heart by using the myocardial oxygen equation: $MVO_2 = 0.14(DP) - 6.3$ and demonstrate that the elevated DP correlates with an elevated MVO_2. At the original resting DP of 84, MVO_2 is 5.46 mL·100 g LV·min^{-1}. But, with the increase in DP to 252, the client's MVO_2 is now 28.98 mL·100 g LV·min^{-1}, which is 5.31 times higher than it should be at rest. Given that the client's coronary arteries are occluded by disease and/or inflammation, the chances increase substantially that he will have a heart attack (i.e., myocardial infarction).

Now, I could dismiss the likelihood of pathology and carry on with the notion of "No pain, no gain". What do you think? Of course, the answer is "No!" The following calculation will help you understand. To begin with, I will determine client's oxygen pulse (O_2 pulse), which is VO_2 divided by HR. At rest, the client's VO_2 and HR are on average for a 70 kg man approximately 250 mL·min^{-1} and 70 beats·min^{-1}, respectively. This means the client's O_2 pulse is 3.57 mL·beat^{-1}. Now, if I put the O_2 pulse value in the stroke volume equation (SV, i.e., the volume of blood ejected per beat) to estimate SV, we will see that his SV is approximately 72 mL·beat^{-1}.

Then, I stopped to say,

> "My point is this: With the client's sensation of chest pain and his feeling of weakness, his HR is expected to be increased well above the usual resting value. For example, if it is 120 beats·min^{-1}, then O$_2$ pulse is decreased to 2.08 mL·beat^{-1}. That means his SV is decreased to 65 mL·beat^{-1}, given that a good estimate of the client's SV = 5.22 x O$_2$ pulse + 53. Again, since the client's resting HR is 120 beats·min^{-1} and his SV is 65 mL·beat^{-1}, his cardiac output (Q) is about 7.8 L·min^{-1} versus the normal average of 5 L·min^{-1} for a resting untrained 70 kg man. The elevated Q is another reason for the tendency to experience chest pain, especially when the coronary arteries cannot supply the blood to the myocardium as they should."

Then, as we were parting ways I said, "If you are going to push your clients, it is important to understand the physiology of prescribing exercise medicine."

Final Thoughts

Chronic diseases are only going to increase without a serious exercise medicine intervention. The aging of the population and the sedentary lifestyle contribute to higher rates of blood pressure, diabetes, and heart disease. Exercise medicine prescribed by the ASEP Board Certified Exercise Physiologist along with changes in sedentary lifestyle represent the most logical intervention both at a personal level and collectively by society. Regardless of age, everyone should begin an exercise medicine program to reduce the risk of increased visits to the doctor's office, hospitalization, and medical costs. It is a challenge but a necessity to change everyday living, eating, and working habits. Otherwise, chronic diseases and disabilities will continue to take their toll on performing basic activities of daily living. The most important answer to this increasing health problem is Exercise Medicine.

References

1 Sharlach, M. (2013). The Exercise Pill: A Better Prescription than Drugs for Patients with Heart Problems? (Online). http://scopeblog.stanford.edu/2013/10/01/the-exercise-pill-a-better-prescription-than-drugs-for-patients-with-heart-problems/.
2 Reynolds, G. (2013). Exercise in a Pill? The Search Continues. (Online). https://well.blogs.nytimes.com/2013/07/17/exercise-in-a-pill-the-search-continues/.
3 Jolla, L. (2017). Exercise-in-a-Pill Boosts Athletic Endurance by 70 Percent. (Online). www.eurekalert.org/pub_releases/2017-05/si-Ba042817.php.
4 U.S. Department of Health and Human Services. (2008). Physical Activity Guidelines for Americans: Be Active, Healthy, and Happy! (Online). http://health.gov/paguidelines/pdf/paguide.pdf.

5 Employee Benefit Research Institute. (2000). *Prescription Drug Costs Up Sharply—but Still Small Overall, Press Release 470* (Washington, DC: EBRI, 1999); and *Consumer Price Index—All Urban Consumers* (Washington, DC: U.S. Department of Commerce, Bureau of Labor Statistics, 2000).
6 Asby, D. J., Cuda, F., Beyaert, M., Houghton, F. D., Cagampang, F. R., & Tavassoli, A. (2015). AMPK Activation via Modulation of De Novo Purine Biosynthesis with an Inhibitor of ATIC Homodimerization. *Chemistry & Biology*. 22, 7: 838–848.
7 Li, S., & Laher, I. (2015). "Exercise Pills: At the Starting Line". Trends in Pharmacological Sciences. (Online). DOI:10.1016/j.tips.2015.08.014.
8 Narkar, V. A., Downes, M., Yu, R. T., Embler, E., Wang, Y. X., Banayo, E., et al. (2008). AMPK and PPARδ Agonists Are Exercise Mimetics. *Cell*. 134, 3: 405–415. (Online). www.cell.com/abstract/S0092-8674(08)00838-36.
9 Wikipedia, The Free Encyclopedia. (2015). GW501516. (Online). https://en.wikipedia.org/wiki/GW501516.
10 de Neef, M. (2013). The New EPO? — GW1516, AICAR and Their Use in Cycling, CyclingTips. (Online). http://cyclingtips.com.au/2013/04/the-new-epo-gw1516-aicar-and-their-use-in-cycling/.
11 Boone, T. (2014). *Introduction to Exercise Physiology*. Burlington, MA: Jones and Bartlett Learning.
12 Boone, T. (2015). *Promoting Professionalism in Exercise Physiology*. Lewiston, NY: The Edwin Mellen Press.
13 Boone, T. (2009). *The Professionalization of Exercise Physiology: Certification, Accreditation, and Standards of Practice of the American Society of Exercise Physiologists (ASEP)*. Lewiston, NY: The Edwin Mellen Press.
14 Boone, T. (2006). *Is Sports Nutrition for Sale?* Hauppauge, NY: Nova Science Publishing.
15 Boone, T. (2014). Dare I Say It: Exercise Medicine. *Professionalization of Exercise Physiology-online*. 17, 4: 1–6.
16 Boone, T. (2015). Physiology of Exercise Medicine. *Journal of Professional Exercise Physiology*. 13, 5: 1–4.
17 Padilla, J., Simmons, G., Bender, S. B., et al. (2011). Vascular Effects of Exercise: Endothelial Adaptations beyond Active Muscle Beds. *Physiology*. 26, 3: 132–145.
18 Ross, M. D., Malone, E., & Florida-James, G. (2016). Vascular Aging and Exercise: Focus on Cellular Reparative Processes. *Oxidative Medicine and Cellular Longevity*. Article ID 3583956, 15 pages. Hindawi Publishing Corporation.
19 Boone, T. (2017). *ASEP's Exercise Medicine Text for Exercise Physiologists*. Beijing, China: Bentham Science Publishing.

10

HEALTHCARE PROVIDER

> Only through a radical shift in our undergraduate degree title and curriculum can exercise physiologists succeed in this new era. It calls for nothing but a complete break with the tradition-bound ways and thinking of the academic exercise physiology teachers and researchers of the present-day age.

"Please tell me how I can become a Board Certified Exercise Physiologist" is a common email received by the ASEP National Office. The desire to be a healthcare provider after graduating from college is a strong breakthrough mentality. Yes, it is taking its sweet time. However, when the faculty realizes that the undergraduate exercise physiology curriculum must be updated to graduate healthcare providers and not personal trainers and/or fitness instructors, exercise physiologists will start thinking differently. After all, what student isn't interested in graduating and finding a great job or creating the job they have always wanted with a great salary? Isn't that what a college degree is about?

Many college administrators have worked well with the faculty to develop some amazing academic majors that do in fact help students become successful in finding good jobs after college. But, unfortunately, there are many meaningless degree programs without the opportunity of a career-specific job. While this may be obvious to some exercise physiologists, it certainly is not understood by thousands of young men and women who are taking undergraduate courses throughout the United States. If they knew the critical issues before the faculty and the degree programs, would they continue to waste their time, money, and future or would they transition to another degree program elsewhere on campus?

> The ASEP exercise physiologists are bound together by a shared professional commitment to being good healthcare providers, taking good care of their clients and patients, and promoting professionalism in exercise physiology.

The Students' Dilemma

To press the point a step further, what is the value in majoring in exercise science or kinesiology when the majority of the college advisors encourage students who are about to graduate to complete an application for graduate school or physical therapy? I have heard faculty members share such conversations for decades. Often the student will say, "But, I am not interested in being a physical therapist or spending more money to get a master's degree." Then, the advisor says, "You will when you can't find a job." For a moment the student sits quietly in the front of the advisor, then, you hear the comment: "Are you saying there are no jobs in exercise science?"

The most common response by many college advisors is, "Well, you can always get certified as a personal trainer, fitness instructor, or even an exercise specialist." I have heard students say, "Certified! Why get certified? You do know I am already a personal trainer, right?" After taking a few breaths, you can hear the advisor say to John at the door, "Come in. Take a seat over there. I will help you complete the PT application in a minute." After taking his eyes off John, Bob looks at his advisor and says, "Really, you are going to help John apply to PT and not help me get a job!" After another deep breath, Bob says in desperation, "I don't understand. This isn't right. My parents are expecting me to get a job that pays well and has health insurance benefits."

A major difference exists between the public's view of college and the reality of why it actually exists. There is one thing that is very important, and that is doing research and publishing papers. College teachers must publish to survive and gain approval and financial support to travel to meetings, to purchase new laboratory equipment, and to get a reduction in the number of courses they are supposed to teach.

> Recently, a college graduate was heard asking a friend: Where are the jobs? Where is the money? Where are the increased opportunities?

Either the lack of interest in professionalism and ethical thinking is real or the faculty simply refuses to acknowledge the students' dilemma. Apparently, they have turned a blind eye to the students' needs. That is why they don't even think about the students' problems and yet, the students and their parents suffer in major ways when college graduates go back home to live.

The purpose of getting a college degree is not complicated. High school graduates go to college with the expectation of transitioning from college into a reasonably good and financially-secure career in which they can begin to build their future. Yet, it is clear that increasingly more college graduates are living with their mom and dad or their aunt and/or uncle. Jordan Weissmann, editor at *The Atlantic*, says, "... the number of college graduates living at home or with grandparents is 45%" (1).

While widely accepted as the norm, the way in which the college faculty operates to empower itself must change. The academic institution does not exist just for the faculty to publish research papers. It is an institution to educate the students, so they will have a much better opportunity at life. The "teachers" are responsible for teaching and caring for their students, which means encouraging creative thinking, incorporating flexible ideas and concepts (such as exercise medicine), integrating the teaching of business and entrepreneurial fundamentals, empowering individual students, replacing competition with trust and support, and sharing the ASEP vision of a better future for all exercise physiologists.

Exercise physiology students need the ability to demonstrate not just the mastery of the subject area, but the drive and business knowledge necessary to start their own exercise medicine clinics. This is the 21st century where it is vital that students know how to achieve their economic goals. The ASEP accredited exercise physiology degree is a healthcare major that sets the stage to graduate Board Certified Exercise Physiologists as healthcare providers to help prevent and manage chronic lifestyle-related diseases and disabilities (2).

The future of all exercise physiologists demands a vision of our academic institutions as creatively evolving for all the students. The faculty can publish their work, but also support the excitement and rewards of the students' success by being the teachers they were hired to be. This is an entirely new vision of why the academic institutions exist, and it is a compelling vision to return to the way it used to be before the emphasis on more and more research and grant money.

To move beyond the limited mentality of how the administrators and faculty think about academia requires the conscious decision to support the work of ASEP in providing the professional infrastructure for exercise physiology to grow as a new healthcare provider. This includes supporting the ASEP vision and the professional meetings. It also means promoting the ASEP accredited exercise physiology degree programs throughout the academic institutions in the United States. We, as individuals, must assume responsibility for our own professional transformation.

The Practice of Exercise Physiology

In addition to the students graduating with a solid education in exercise medicine, the world of entrepreneurialism will be the exercise physiologists' transition into full healthcare recognition and employment. With the exercise medicine-based approach to healthcare, the practice of exercise physiology by Board Certified Exercise Physiologists will be applied to healthy individuals as well as individuals with known chronic diseases and/or ill-health (3). The goals for such practice are to:

1. Promote mental and physical health and wellness.
2. Improve the components of physical fitness (that includes muscle strength, endurance, and flexibility and cardiorespiratory performance).
3. Prevent disease and disability (via the identification of risk factors and behaviors that may impede mind-body functioning).
4. Assist in restoring health and well-being to clients with disease and/or disability.
5. Rehabilitate clients to their optimal functional level following physical and/or mental illness.

The equipment used in the practice of exercise physiology may include the use of submaximal and maximal testing using treadmills and various cycle ergometers to make evaluations and recommendations regarding, but not limited to, metabolic processes, the cardiorespiratory system, the musculoskeletal system (strength and power tests), and body composition (% body fat tests).

The measurement, examination, analysis, and instruction will be done for the purpose of research, counsel, and improvement of the client's physical and emotional well-being, including improvement in factors that lead to increased athletic performance. Nothing in the above description authorizes the Board Certified Exercise Physiologist to diagnose disease either by using the ECG (i.e., electrocardiogram) or by any means resulting from exercise physiology laboratory procedures (4).

However, due to the use of exercise as a diagnostic tool in many medical fields, ASEP Board Certified Exercise Physiologist may be used by the medical personnel to conduct tests that assist in the medical diagnosis of disease. Having concluded that Board Certified Exercise Physiologists do not diagnose disease or perform clinical services that infringe on the practice of others does not preclude the right to identify and discuss signs and symptoms of disease that otherwise correlate with physical limitations and/or clinical dysfunctions.

> The right combination of physiological data provides the essential information that will help the exercise physiologists further understand and explain the client's responses at rest and during either a constant submaximal workload or a progressive workload.

Also, it is recommended that the exercise testing of clients with known risk factors for coronary artery disease should be performed with the supervision (or approval) of a medical doctor who is responsible for ensuring that the exercise laboratory is equipped to handle emergencies. Understandably, the physician is ultimately responsible for interpreting the ECG data from testing, and any timely administration of drugs, defibrillation (if required), and any other appropriate medication resulting from or associated with the test. The ASEP Board Certified Exercise Physiologist is responsible for the following:

1. Initiating and assisting in the supervision of the exercise laboratory and personnel.
2. Preparing the client and/or patient for the placement of electrodes.
3. Taking a resting blood pressure and 12-lead ECG strips.
4. Determining the exercise ECG response to the exercise protocol.
5. Ruling out any contraindications to continuing the test.

The ASEP Board Certified Exercise Physiologist is also responsible for acknowledging the scientific and medical findings that associate with the clients' diseases and/or dysfunctions along with the appropriate language for sharing the same (i.e., primary and secondary risk factors) with the client when monitoring his or her cardiorespiratory status while using exercise and/or metabolic equipment to determine oxygen consumption (VO_2) and related hemodynamic responses (heart rate, HR; blood pressure, BP; cardiac output, Q; stroke volume, SV; arteriovenous oxygen difference, a-vO_2 diff; double product, DP; and myocardial oxygen consumption, MVO_2) throughout the exercise and recovery periods, and instructing the client as to how he or she should prepare for the test (4).

Testing for symptom-limited maximum oxygen consumption (primarily in post-myocardial infarction patients) or maximum oxygen consumption (VO_2 max, the greatest amount of oxygen a person can use when performing dynamic exercise involving a large muscle mass) is an important test to identify and discuss signs and symptoms that might associate with disease and/or dysfunction. VO_2 max represents the amount of oxygen transported and used at the muscle tissue level in cellular metabolism. It is the product of maximum cardiac output (Q) and maximum arteriovenous oxygen difference (i.e., tissue extraction of O_2). Since Q is equal to the product of heart rate (HR) and stroke volume (SV), the test helps to evaluate the role of both in the transport of blood to the peripheral tissues (4).

Myocardial oxygen uptake (MVO_2) is determined by the Board Certified Exercise Physiologist through the use of a regression formula, such as [MVO_2 = 0.14 (HR x SBP x 0.01) − 6.3]. The product of HR and systolic blood pressure (SBP) is called double product (DP). It is a linear relation between MVO_2 and coronary blood flow. During exercise, HR increases linearly with the client's workload and VO_2. Systolic blood pressure rises with increased work as a result of the increase in Q while diastolic blood pressure usually remains the same or decreases somewhat. The failure of SBP to rise with exercise can be the result of aortic outflow obstruction, left ventricular dysfunction, or myocardial ischemia. The changes in blood pressure may also reflect peripheral vascular resistance, given that systemic vascular resistance (SVR) equals mean arterial pressure (MAP) divided by Q. Given that the client's Q is expected to increase with the progressive increments in exercise and MAP usually changes very little, then, SVR is expected to decrease with exercise (4).

Measurement and Evaluation

The Board Certified Exercise Physiologist's role in measurement and examination includes: (a) the administration of a health history questionnaire, a disease-specific or disorder-specific laboratory evaluation, as well as the assessment of the musculoskeletal system and/or the cardiorespiratory system using various metabolic analyzers, exercise tests protocols, exercise programs, and risk factor modification and/or measurements to assist in evaluating overt and/or objective responses, signs, and/or symptoms of a cardiorespiratory fitness test, body composition, range of motion (flexibility), and muscle strength of a client who is either apparently healthy or who has disease; (b) the administration of a pulmonary function test and exercise prescription for cardiorespiratory fitness of a client with metabolic disorders including, but not limited to, deficiencies of the cardiovascular system, diabetes, lipid disorders, hypertension, cancer, cystic fibrosis, chronic obstructive and restrictive pulmonary diseases, arthritis, organ transplant, peripheral vascular disease, and obesity; and (c) analysis of the exercise ergometer tests in conjunction with exercise electrocardiography (ECG) to identify the heart rate and ECG responses at rest and during submaximal and maximal graded exercise and the acknowledgment of specific contraindications, if any, for continuing to exercise.

The exercise physiology examination does not include examining a client for the purpose of diagnosing disease or organic condition, as though the Board Certified Exercise Physiologist has licensure to do so. However, nothing herein is intended to preclude Board Certified Exercise Physiologists from supervising a stress test and/or using different ergometers in the assessment and determination of the cause of a problem, particularly when it comes to educating, consulting, and supervising a client.

Ultimately, this thinking helps to drive ASEP's accreditation and promote ASEP Board Certification that should be part of the exercise medicine intervention. Thus, it should be self-evident that educating clients as to how and why the body responds to a safe prescription of regular exercise helps in promoting a healthy lifestyle. In short, education is at the heart of the healthcare change process.

Clients do not need to know everything about different diseases and how exercise helps in staying healthy. But, they do need to keep their mental process engaged to help facilitate an understanding of the physiological changes that result from the new exercise medicine lifestyle. Indeed, coping and adapting to a new way of living is not an isolated event, but rather a new mental and physical homeostasis. Also, in response to the exercise-induced cardiorespiratory and skeletal muscle responses, the metabolic stress of regular exercise promotes positive changes in the brain and mental response to daily stressors.

Mind–body crosstalk is intimately linked to the ASEP's message to educate clients. The emphasis on education is critical to the 21st century view of the Board Certified

Exercise Physiologists' role in healthcare throughout the United States. As an example, given that the typical college graduate does not have the money to purchase expensive metabolic analyzers, several regression equations are presented to help the client understand why exercise medicine should be prescribed by an exercise physiologist.

Please appreciate this content is presented to demonstrate just how much information and insight is possible with using this approach when helping the client grasp an understanding of exercise medicine. Much more can be said about each physiologic response and how each relates to other responses. The beauty of this beginning is once the client is introduced to, for example, oxygen consumption and what it means, then, the door is open to thinking about other related physiological responses.

Oxygen Consumption

The oxygen consumption (VO_2) in $mL \cdot min^{-1}$ of the client can be calculated from the kilopond meters ($kpm \cdot min^{-1}$) of workload on a Monark cycle ergometer using Equation 1. In this case, the client is exercising at 600 $kpm \cdot min^{-1}$ (or a 100 Watts, given 600 ÷ 6 = 100) that requires a VO_2 of 1500 $mL \cdot min^{-1}$ or 1.5 $L \cdot min^{-1}$. With just a brief conversation, the client can come to understand the importance of oxygen during exercising by speaking to the VO_2 to sustain the workload.

$$\begin{aligned} VO_2 \ (mL \cdot min^{-1}) &= (kpm \cdot min^{-1} \times 2) + 300 \\ &= (600 \times 2) + 300 \\ &= 1500 \ mL \cdot min^{-1} \ (or \ 1.5 \ L \cdot min^{-1}) \end{aligned}$$

(1)

Kilocalories

While it is not important for the client to know the specific steps in the citric acid cycle or the way in which adenosine triphosphate (ATP) sustains muscle contraction, he or she should have a basic understanding of what is happening in the body. For example, the client should know that at a given VO_2, he is expending "x" number of $kcal \cdot min^{-1}$ (refer to Equation 2).

$$\begin{aligned} kcal \cdot min^{-1} &= VO_2 \ (L \cdot min^{-1}) \times 5 \\ &= 1.5 \times 5 \\ &= 7.5 \ kcal \cdot min^{-1} \ (times \ 20 \ min \ of \ cycling = 150 \ kcal) \end{aligned}$$

(2)

Cardiac Output

Remember, as a healthcare professional, you are doing what you can to motivate your clients to stay with the exercise medicine program. Given that the estimated exercise VO_2 in $L \cdot min^{-1}$ at 600 $kpm \cdot min^{-1}$, cardiac output (Q) can be discussed using Equation 3. The 12.58 $L \cdot min^{-1}$ is increased 2½ times relative to the average resting cardiac output of 5 $L \cdot min^{-1}$.

$$\begin{aligned}
Q\ (L \cdot min^{-1}) &= (6.12 \times VO_2\ L \cdot min^{-1}) + 3.4 \\
&= (6.12 \times 1.5\ L \cdot min^{-1}) + 3.4 \\
&= 12.58\ L \cdot min^{-1}
\end{aligned}$$

(3)

Arteriovenous Oxygen Difference

Knowing the client's exercise VO_2 and Q at 600 $kpm \cdot min^{-1}$ allows for talking about extraction of oxygen (a-vO_2 diff) by the muscles for the continuation of muscle contraction and, therefore, the cycle ergometer exercise itself. The value is little more than two times the resting tissue extraction (refer to Equation 4).

$$\begin{aligned}
\text{a-}vO_2\ \text{diff}\ (mL \cdot dL^{-1}) &= [VO_2\ (L \cdot min^{-1}) \div Q\ (L \cdot min^{-1})] \times 100 \\
&= [1.5\ L \cdot min^{-1} \div 12.58\ L \cdot min^{-1}] \times 100 \\
&= 11.92\ mL \cdot dL^{-1}
\end{aligned}$$

(4)

Stroke Volume

Similarly, with respect to Equation 5, knowing the client's exercise heart rate (HR), the volume of blood ejected from the heart per beat (stroke volume, SV) into the arterial blood can be estimated.

$$\begin{aligned}
SV\ (mL \cdot bt^{-1}) &= Q\ (mL \cdot min^{-1}) \div HR\ (beats \cdot min^{-1}) \\
&= 12{,}580\ mL \cdot min^{-1} \div 100\ beats \cdot min^{-1} \\
&= 125.8\ mL \cdot bt^{-1}
\end{aligned}$$

(5)

Double Product

Also, a brief analysis of the client's double product at rest (Equation 6) and during exercise will help in understanding the work of the heart, given that DP is correlated with myocardial oxygen consumption (MVO_2) (Equation 7).

$$\begin{aligned}
DP &= HR\ (beats \cdot min^{-1}) \times SBP\ (mmHg) \times 0.01 \\
&= (70\ beats \cdot min^{-1} \times 120\ mmHg) \times 0.01 \\
&= 8400 \times 0.01 \\
&= 84\ (\text{at rest})
\end{aligned}$$

(6)

Myocardial Oxygen Consumption

$$MVO_2 \text{ (mL·100 g LV·min}^{-1}) = 0.14 \text{ (HR x SBP x 0.01)} - 6.3$$
$$= 0.14 \text{ (70 x 120 x 0.01)} - 6.3$$
$$= 0.14 \text{ (84)} - 6.3$$
$$= 5.46 \text{ mL·100 g LV·min}^{-1} \text{ (at rest)}$$

(7)

Here, it is important to point out to the client that his or her commitment to daily exercise has resulted in positive physiological changes in heart rate (HR) and systolic blood pressure (SBP) during exercise (Equation 8). The changes allow the heart to do the same amount of work while requiring less oxygen. Thus, a positive effect of training is that as the heart supplies oxygen to the peripheral tissues via left ventricular contraction, it does so in a more efficient manner.

$$MVO_2 \text{ (mL·100 g LV·min}^{-1}) = 0.14 \text{ (HR x SBP x 0.01)} - 6.3$$
$$= 0.14 \text{ (140 x 180 x 0.01)} - 6.3$$
$$= 29 \text{ mL·100 g LV·min}^{-1} \text{ (exercise before training)}$$

$$MVO_2 \text{ (mL·100 g LV·min}^{-1}) = 0.14 \text{ (HR x SBP x 0.01)} - 6.3$$
$$= 0.14 \text{ (120 x 165 x 0.01)} - 6.3$$
$$= 21 \text{ mL·100 g LV·min}^{-1} \text{ (exercise after training)}$$

(8)

Heart Weight

The following calculations (Equations 9–12) will help the client understand the relationship between the size of the heart and his or her body weight. The weight of the heart is larger in men versus women. Using the data in Equation 9 with respect to HR, SBP, and MVO_2 (mL·100 g LV·min^{-1}), absolute MVO_2 (in mL·min^{-1}) can be estimated via the following equations.

$$HW_{men} \text{ (g)} = (2.54 \text{ x kgBW)} + 128 = (2.54 \text{ x 70 kg)} + 128 = 306 \text{ g}$$

(9)

$$HW_{women} \text{ (g)} = (2.10 \text{ x kgBW)} + 126 = (2.10 \text{ x 60 kg)} + 126 = 252 \text{ g}$$

(10)

$$MVO_{2men} \text{ (mL·min}^{-1}) = MVO_2 \text{ (mL·100 g LV·min}^{-1}) \text{ x HWF}$$
$$= 5.46 \text{ mL·100 g LV·min}^{-1} \text{ x 3.06 g}$$
$$= 16.7 \text{ mL·min}^{-1}$$

(11)

$$\text{MVO}_{2\text{women}} \text{ (mL·min}^{-1}\text{)} = \text{MVO}_2 \text{ (mL·100 g LV·min}^{-1}\text{)} \times \text{HWF}$$
$$= \star 7.14 \text{ mL·100 g LV·min}^{-1} \times 2.52 \text{ g}$$
$$= 17.99 \text{ mL·min}^{-1}$$

(12)

Assuming a resting HR of 80 in women (vs. 70 in men) at the same SBP of 120 mmHg, the MVO_2 for women would be 7.14 mL·100 g LV·min^{-1}. But, since 17 and 18 mL·min^{-1} are essentially the same, the increase in HR to deal with the smaller SV in women means that both men and women consume about equal amounts of oxygen at the heart level.

Left Ventricular Power Output

The client's left ventricular power output (LVPO) can be calculated using the cardiac output regression formula, Q (L·min^{-1}) = (6.12 x VO_2 L·min^{-1}) + 3.4 and measuring blood pressure.

$$\text{LVPO (kg·m·min}^{-1}\text{)} = \text{Q (L·min}^{-1}\text{)} \times \text{SBP (mmHg)} \times 13.6 \times 0.001$$
$$= 9.52 \text{ L·min}^{-1} \times 150 \text{ mmHg} \times 13.6 \times 0.001$$
$$= 19.42 \text{ kg·m·min}^{-1} \text{ [at 300 kpm·min}^{-1}\text{]}$$

$$\text{LVPO (kg·m·min}^{-1}\text{)} = \text{Q (L·min}^{-1}\text{)} \times \text{SBP (mmHg)} \times 13.6 \times 0.001$$
$$= 12.58 \text{ L·min}^{-1} \times 175 \text{ mmHg} \times 13.6 \times 0.001$$
$$= 29.94 \text{ kg·m·min}^{-1} \text{ [at 600 kpm·min}^{-1}\text{]}$$

$$\text{LVPO (kg·m·min}^{-1}\text{)} = \text{Q (L·min}^{-1}\text{)} \times \text{SBP (mmHg)} \times 13.6 \times 0.001$$
$$= 16.25 \text{ L·min}^{-1} \times 195 \text{ mmHg} \times 13.6 \times 0.001$$
$$= 43.01 \text{ kg·m·min}^{-1} \text{ [at 900 kpm·min}^{-1}\text{]}$$

(13)

Cardiac Power Output

Then, the exercise physiologist can talk about cardiac power output (CPO), which is LVPO plus the power output of the right ventricle (Equation 14).

$$\text{CPO (kg·m·min}^{-1}\text{)} = \text{LVPO} \times 1.2$$
$$= 19.42 \text{ kg·m·min}^{-1} \times 1.2$$
$$= 23.30 \text{ kg·m·min}^{-1} \text{ [at 300 kpm·min}^{-1}\text{]}$$

$$\text{CPO (kg·m·min}^{-1}\text{)} = \text{LVPO} \times 1.2$$
$$= 29.94 \text{ kg·m·min}^{-1} \times 1.2$$
$$= 35.92 \text{ kg·m·min}^{-1} \text{ [at 600 kpm·min}^{-1}\text{]}$$

$$\text{CPO (kg·m·min}^{-1}\text{)} = \text{LVPO} \times 1.2$$

$$= 43.01 \text{ kg·m·min}^{-1} \times 1.2$$
$$= 51.62 \text{ kg·m·min}^{-1} \text{ [at 900 kpm·min}^{-1}\text{]}$$
(14)

Given that the weight of the average male heart is ~300 g, the mass of the left ventricle is ~180 g (due to the ventricular contraction against a relatively high mean arterial pressure due to ventricular systole that is in part driven by the high systemic vascular resistance) while the mass of the right ventricle is ~60 g (due to less contractile work to send the blood to the lungs via the pulmonary arteries). This leaves ~20 g each for both of the upper chambers

Mean Arterial Pressure

The mean arterial pressure (MAP, Equation 15) and the systemic vascular resistance (SVR, Equation 16) can be discussed using the following regression formulae. Note that MAP rises with the increase in systolic blood pressure, which is appropriate given the increase in the client's exercise intensity along with the decrease in the SVR.

$$\text{MAP (mmHg)} = \text{DBP} + 0.32 \text{ (pulse pressure, i.e., SBP} - \text{DBP)}$$
$$= 80 \text{ mmHg} + 0.32 \text{ (120 mmHg} - 80 \text{ mmHg)}$$
$$= 80 + 0.32 \text{ (40)}$$
$$= 93 \text{ mmHg [at rest]}$$

$$= 80 \text{ mmHg} + 0.32 \text{ (150 mmHg} - 80 \text{ mmHg)}$$
$$= 80 \text{ mmHg} + 0.32 \text{ (65)}$$
$$= 101 \text{ mmHg [at 300 kpm·min}^{-1}\text{; 50 Watts]}$$

$$= 70 \text{ mmHg} + 0.32 \text{ (175 mmHg} - 70 \text{ mmHg)}$$
$$= 70 \text{ mmHg} + 0.32 \text{ (105)}$$
$$= 104 \text{ mmHg [at 600 kpm·min}^{-1}\text{; 100 Watts]}$$

$$= 70 \text{ mmHg} + 0.32 \text{ (195 mmHg} - 70 \text{ mmHg)}$$
$$= 70 \text{ mmHg} + 0.32 \text{ (125)}$$
$$= 114 \text{ mmHg [at 900 kpm·min}^{-1}\text{; 150 Watts]}$$
(15)

Systemic Vascular Resistance

Systemic vascular resistance (SVR) refers to the resistance to blood flow that is due to the systemic vasculature. It is also referred to as total peripheral resistance (TPR). In brief, any condition that causes peripheral vasoconstriction increases SVR, and any conditions that cause vasodilation decrease SVR. Although SVR is primarily determined by changes in blood vessel diameters, changes in blood viscosity can also influence SVR. SVR can be calculated if cardiac output (CO), mean arterial pressure (MAP), and cardiac output (Q) are known (Equation 16).

$$\text{SVR (mmHg·L·min}^{-1}) = \text{MAP (mmHg)} \div Q \text{ (L·min}^{-1})$$
$$= 93 \text{ mmHg} \div 5 \text{ L·min}^{-1}$$
$$= 18.6 \text{ mmHg·L·min}^{-1} \text{ [at rest]}$$

$$\text{SVR (mmHg·L·min}^{-1}) = \text{MAP (mmHg)} \div Q \text{ (L·min}^{-1})$$
$$= 101 \text{ mmHg} \div 9.52 \text{ L·min}^{-1}$$
$$= 10.6 \text{ mmHg·L·min}^{-1} \text{ [at 300 kpm·min}^{-1}\text{]}$$

$$\text{SVR (mmHg·L·min}^{-1}) = \text{MAP (mmHg)} \div Q \text{ (L·min}^{-1})$$
$$= 104 \text{ mmHg} \div 12.58 \text{ L·min}^{-1}$$
$$= 8.26 \text{ mmHg·L·min}^{-1} \text{ [at 600 kpm·min}^{-1}\text{]}$$

$$\text{SVR (mmHg·L·min}^{-1}) = \text{MAP (mmHg)} \div Q \text{ (L·min}^{-1})$$
$$= 114 \text{ mmHg} \div 16.25 \text{ L·min}^{-1}$$
$$= 7.01 \text{ mmHg·L·min}^{-1} \text{ [at 900 kpm·min}^{-1}\text{]}$$

(16)

While the use of estimates of the client's physiologic responses to exercising is not as accurate as actual measurements determined through the use of various testing modalities, ASEP Board Certified Exercise Physiologists should use them to educate the client in understanding oxygen consumption and related physiological variables and responses to exercise medicine training.

The beauty of the ownership of the exercise physiology concepts, principles, and ideas is that once you have established the application of these formulae and/or similar information, it helps in demonstrating the physiology that undergirds exercise medicine and its application in one's own healthcare business. What's more, starting one's own exercise medicine clinic will help promote the exercise physiologist's financial status, which is a game changer when it comes to not finding a credible career opportunity after college.

Please keep in mind that recently graduated exercise physiologists do not generally have access to open circuit spirometry and other expensive laboratory equipment. Therefore, the standardized metabolic equations presented in this chapter can be routinely used to estimate the client and/or patient's physiological responses at rest and during the cycle ergometer exercise. This information can be shared with client in the form of educating him or her to what is taking place in the body during exercise. In so doing, the client can begin to comprehend the responses and adaptations that occur with regular exercise (as they enjoy a better quality of life).

Instruction

Exercise physiology instruction includes providing educational, consultative, and other advisory services for the purpose of helping the client with issues and concerns regarding fundamental and scientific information about mind-body health and fitness (3). Instruction pertains to matters that are believed to develop, maintain, and improve the client's health, fitness, rehabilitation, and/or athletic performance, which might include one or more of the following:

1. Acute physiological responses to exercise.
2. Chronic physiological adaptations to training.
3. Designing resistance training programs.
4. Measuring energy expenditure at rest and during exercise.
5. Hormonal regulation and/or metabolic adaptations to training.
6. Cardiorespiratory regulation and adaptation during exercise.
7. Thermal regulation during exercise.
8. Exercising at altitude, underwater, and in space.
9. Optimizing sports training through the use of better nutrition.
10. Appropriate body composition and optimal body weight and the role each plays in diabetes and physical activity.
11. Growth and development of young athletes, aging, and gender issues.
12. Preventing cardiovascular disease through exercise, the prescription of exercise for increased health, well-being, and performance.
13. Biomechanical assessment of posture and movement.
14. Stress testing protocols for athletics and special populations.
15. Psychophysiological techniques for reducing stress and anxiety.
16. Mind and body benefits of exercise medicine.

Analysis and Treatment

The Board Certified Exercise Physiologist's analysis and treatment includes performing laboratory tests with specific expectations to analyze and treat the client's condition (3,4). This may include, but not limited to, the following:

1. Range of motion (flexibility) exercises.
2. Muscle strength and muscle endurance exercises.
3. Lean muscle tissue-fat analysis.
4. Musculoskeletal and/or postural exercises.
5. Sports nutrition assessment.
6. Sports biomechanics instructions for the enhancement of occupational or sports related skills.
7. Stress management exercises.
8. Sports training programs.
9. Cardiac and/or pulmonary rehabilitation (including, but not limited to, the development of such programs, supervising testing, development of the exercise prescription, and other functions such as the disease-specific education and counseling of patients).

10. Exercise physiology instruction that pertains to all forms of sports training and athletics.

Code of Ethics

The significance of the Code of Ethics for Board Certified Exercise Physiologists (5) is that both students and professionals in the study and application of exercise physiology to health, fitness, exercise, preventive, and rehabilitative services can turn to it for guidance in professional conduct. Adherence to the Code is expected of all ASEP Board Certified Exercise Physiologists. It is based on the belief that exercise physiologists are self-regulated critical thinkers who are healthcare providers responsible for their high-quality competence in the practice of exercise physiology concepts, ideas, and services.

Board Certified exercise physiologists should accurately communicate and provide health and fitness, educational, preventive, rehabilitative, and/or research services equitably to all individuals regardless of social or economic status, age, gender, race, ethnicity, national origin, religion, disability, diverse values, attitudes, or opinions. They should be responsible and accountable for individual non-medical judgments and decisions about health and fitness, preventive, rehabilitative, educational, and/or research services.

1. Exercise physiologists should accurately communicate and provide health and fitness, educational, preventive, rehabilitative, and/or research services equitably to all individuals regardless of social or economic status, age, gender, race, ethnicity, national origin, religion, disability, diverse values, attitudes, or opinions.
2. Exercise physiologists should be responsible and accountable for individual non-medical judgments and decisions about health and fitness, preventive, rehabilitative, educational, and/or research services.
3. Exercise physiologists should maintain high quality professional competence through continued study of the latest laboratory techniques and research in preventive and rehabilitative services.
4. Exercise physiologists are expected to conduct health and fitness, preventive, rehabilitative, educational, research, and other scholarly activities in accordance with recognized legal, scientific, ethical, and professional standards.
5. Exercise physiologists should respect and protect the privacy, rights, and dignity of all individuals by not disclosing health and fitness, rehabilitative, and/or research information unless required by law or when confidentiality jeopardizes the health and safety of others.
6. Exercise physiologists are expected to call attention to unprofessional health and fitness, preventive, rehabilitative, educational, and/or research services that result from incompetent, unethical, or illegal professional behavior.
7. Exercise physiologists should contribute to the ongoing development and integrity of the profession by being responsive to, mutually supportive, and accurately communicating academic and other qualifications to colleagues and associates in the health and fitness, preventive, rehabilitative, educational and/or research services and programs.

8. Exercise physiologists should participate in the profession's efforts to establish high quality services by avoiding conflicts of interest and endorsement of products in the health and fitness, preventive, and/or rehabilitative services and programs.
9. Exercise physiologists should participate in and encourage critical discourse to reflect the collective knowledge and practice within the exercise physiology profession to protect the public from misinformation, incompetence, and unethical acts.
10. Exercise physiologists should provide health and fitness, preventive, rehabilitative, and/or educational interventions grounded in a theoretical framework supported by research that enables a healthy lifestyle through choice.

The ASEP leadership developed the first-ever academic accreditation guidelines for the exercise physiology major and, then, Board Certification that is required before they begin their professional practice. The ASEP leadership understood that many of the non-communicable (chronic) diseases (such as diabetes, colon cancer, osteoarthritis, osteoporosis, and obesity) could be managed by exercise physiologists who are ASEP Board Certified.

When exercise medicine is correctly prescribed, it helps to relieve symptoms of depression and anxiety, thus improving mood and promoting a client's sense of well-being. The ASEP exercise prescription is exercise medicine that should be administered by Board Certified Exercise Physiologists.

ASEP Accreditation

The American Society of Exercise Physiologists was founded in 1997 to unite exercise physiologists and to promote the professional development of exercise physiology (6,7). Thus, it serves to protect the professional well-being of exercise physiologists by enhancing the recognition of their work and educating the public as to their role in athletics, fitness, allied health, rehabilitation, and medical programs.

> The price of change requires your total commitment, mind and body. But then something great happens: True professionalism is lived, and now you are what you believed you were.

Also, ASEP fosters the exchange of ideas and research among exercise physiologists to promote a forum for the advancement of the profession. The First National Meeting was held at The College of St. Scholastica in Duluth, MN in 1998. In addition to the ASEPNewsletter, the ASEP organization publishes four peer reviewed electronic journals:

1. Journal of Exercise Physiology-online
2. Journal of Exercise Medicine-online
3. Professionalization of Exercise Physiology-online
4. Journal of Professional Exercise Physiology

Academic accreditation is necessary to help ensure that the academic programs are well designed to prepare students for the exercise physiology profession. This is important to help prepare the graduating students, so they will have an excellent chance of passing the ASEP Board Certification. Then, the graduates who become Board Certified are held accountable to the ASEP Code of Ethics and Standards of Professional Practice.

Work began on the development of the accreditation program in early 1998. Through the collaborative efforts of exercise physiologists throughout the United States, the accreditation guidelines were submitted for final approval by the Board of Directors at the 1999 National Meeting. The ASEP guidelines represent a compilation of work by exercise physiologists who identified what they believed to be the "standards acceptable for educating students for a career in exercise physiology."

> It takes courage to take a stand against yesterday's thinking. The ASEP Board Certification is a statement of such courage. It is the right strategy, message, and vision of something better for all exercise physiologists.

Academic accreditation is an important and essential component to any profession. The Board of Accreditation works with academic programs to ensure that standards are met and that the graduating students are worthy of the title—Exercise Physiologist. The benefits of academic accreditation are: (a) the public knows that "x" academic programs are critically evaluated and updated to meet the ASEP requirement; (b) the students are better prepared for the Board Certification exam; (c) the public can be confident that the ASEP Board Certified Exercise Physiologists are professionally prepared healthcare providers; and (d) in time, students will gravitate to the ASEP-accredited programs since there will be little incentive to enroll in a program not recognized by ASEP.

The ASEP Board of Accreditation works with the educational institutions to ensure that the graduates entering the exercise physiology profession are professionally prepared. The Board consists of individuals from the various colleges and universities, the cardiopulmonary rehab sector, and the fitness and wellness industry. Their professional expertise and experience in leadership and professionalism provides the assurance that accreditation is fair, reliable, and effective.

Final Thoughts

There is work to be done to bring forth the full message of exercise medicine by exercise physiologists. We can start by acknowledging that our society is in a new age of continuing failure in health and well-being. The inactivity, sedentary lifestyle, obesity, diseases, and disabilities are at an all-time high. The ASEP leaders believe that if the undergraduate exercise physiologists want to be recognized as the healthcare practitioners of choice in prescribing exercise medicine, they must be able to deal with: (a) the power, politics, and greed of exercise physiology colleagues and generic organizations; (b) the uncertainty and unpredictability of the change process; and (c) the importance of educating, engaging, and supporting the students of exercise physiology in the ASEP vision.

Specifically, this means talking about professionalism in exercise physiology, the exercise physiologist's code of ethical thinking, the profession-specific academic accreditation and Board Certification, and the standards of practice for all exercise physiologists from the undergraduate degree through the doctorate degree (7). And yet, strangely enough, there isn't even any research about professionalism from the academic community. There are few college teachers asking, "Why is professionalism in exercise physiology important?"

That being the case, it follows that many exercise physiologists are interested in one thing and that is research and publishing their papers. Of course, it is clear that not just any exercise physiologist can enjoy the benefits of publishing. First, 99% of those who publish exercise physiology research have the doctorate degree. Second, the majority of the doctorate prepared exercise physiologists work in academic institutions where there is research equipment to collect data. Hence, if an exercise physiologist does not have the doctorate degree and does not work in an academic setting, they are not engaged in research.

That said, the future of exercise physiology is exercise medicine carried out by non-doctorate Board Certified Exercise Physiologists. They will emphasize the importance of professional development, code of ethics, and standards of practice as the professional foundation for the prescription of exercise medicine specific to children, adolescents, and adults. An individualized recommendation of 30 minutes or more moderate-intensity physical activity on most, preferably all, days of the week is expected to result in physiologic improvements in strength, endurance, body composition, insulin sensitivity, and lipid levels (8,9).

Board Certified Exercise Physiologists understand the importance of exercise medicine all too well, and they will help clients and patients safely reduce the risk of developing cardiovascular disease, type 2 diabetes, colon cancers, osteoporosis, depression, and fall related injuries (10). They will do so by educating their clients in the "physiology of the exercise responses" that are specific to their health and disease condition (11).

> Board Certified Exercise Physiologists will maintain active responsibility for the growth of the exercise physiology profession and the health and well-being of the individuals they serve by safely prescribing exercise medicine.

References

1 Weissmann, J. (2013). Here's Exactly How Many College Graduates Live at Home. The Atlantic. (Online). www.theatlantic.com/business/archive/2013/02/heres-exactly-how-many-college-graduates-live-back-at-home/273529/.
2 Boone, T. (2016). *ASEP's Exercise Medicine Text for Exercise Physiologists*. Beijing, China: Bentham Science Publishers.
3 Boone, T. (2013). *Exercise Physiology as a Healthcare Profession*. Lewiston, NY: The Edwin Mellen Press.
4 Boone, T. (2013). *Introduction to Exercise Physiology*. Burlington, MA: Jones & Bartlett Learning.
5 American Society of Exercise Physiologists. (2017). Code of Ethics. (Online). wwww.asep.org/index.php/organization/code-ethics/.
6 Boone, T. (2001). *Professional Development of Exercise Physiology*. Lewiston, NY: The Edwin Mellen Press.
7 Boone, T. (2009). *The Professionalization of Exercise Physiology: Certification, accreditation, and standards of practice of the American Society of Exercise Physiologists (ASEP)*. Lewiston, NY: The Edwin Mellen Press.
8 Pate, R. R., Pratt, M., Blair, S. N., et al. (1995). Physical Activity and Public Health. A Recommendation from the Centers for Disease Control and Prevention and the American College of Sports Medicine. *Journal of the American Medical Association*. 273: 402–407.
9 Kahn, E. B., Ramsey, L. T., Brownson, R. C., et al. (2002). The Effectiveness of Interventions to Increase Physical Activity: A Systematic Review. *American Journal of Preventive Medicine*. 22: 73–107.
10 BooneT. (2012). *The Business of Exercise Physiology: Thinking like an entrepreneur*. Lewiston, NY: The Edwin Mellen Press.
11 Boone, T. (2018). The ASEP Exercise Physiologists' Way of Prescribing Exercise Medicine. *Journal of Exercise Physiology-online*. 21, 4: 1–10.

11

TRANSCENDING OUR LIMITS

Some years ago, I realized that

> We must not limit our view of exercise physiology regardless of any past experiences. Instead, we must imagine what exercise physiology can be, and we must transcend our limitations. It is not a question of being a big or a small organization. It is simply a question of sticking to the ASEP vision until it becomes a tangible reality.

I find myself thinking these thoughts several times a week. It helps me to keep my eyes open to the possibilities exercise physiology has for each of us. There cannot be any question that our minds determine our actions, our behavior, and our future. No one is forcing me to think this way, but I believe that we are responsible for our actions. I believe we are the sum of what we think, and that our thoughts shape us. What we talk about determined our destiny and others agree, especially the American motivational speaker, Earl Nightingale (1) who said: "We become what we think about most of the time, and that's the strangest secret."

The Price of Change

The price exercise physiologists are paying to change (i.e., to think of themselves as healthcare providers) is time (2). It takes time to get into shape, to get rid of extra pounds of body fat, and to think differently. It is a big price to pay because time moves so slowly when it comes to professional changes, ethics, and work, and the realty of an accurate representation of what is medicine, what is physical therapy, and what is exercise physiology? The fact that time is lost by the slowness in accepting a new view of exercise physiology provides the opportunity to doubt whether the reasons for change are right.

We should also realize that another price of change influenced by time is the role of the exercise physiologist in exercise medicine and healthcare. The sooner exercise physiologists identify themselves as the exercise medicine providers, the less chance of other professions assuming a leadership role in prescribing exercise medicine. Understanding this point should result in the immediate emphasis placed on professionalism, exercise physiology, and exercise medicine (3).

Board Certified Exercise Physiologists understand the importance of thinking and living as exercise physiology healthcare providers. Yet, in spite of the growth within ASEP to think as a professional, the majority of the exercise physiologists in the United States are not ASEP members. As the billionaire entrepreneur Richard M. DeVos (4) said, "The only thing that stands between a man and what he wants from life is often merely the will to try it and the faith to believe that it is possible." Take a moment and ask yourself the following questions:

1. What is the profile of the "typical" exercise physiologist?
2. What do exercise physiologists do in the public sector?
3. What type of educational preparation is required to become an exercise physiologist?
4. What are the career opportunities and roles that should be developed in society that uses the exercise physiologist's skills in different ways?
5. What keeps the exercise physiologists interested in the ASEP organization and Board Certification?

While attitude towards change makes all the difference, the attitude of most academic exercise physiologists (that was learned during their doctorate degree) is not with regard to professionalism and the growth of exercise physiology. Instead, it is about their personal concerns in playing the academic game of personal survival. Their college professors talked constantly about research and publishing. The doctorate prepared exercise physiologist thinks of him- or herself primarily as a researcher. Teaching is something college teachers do because it is part of the academic position. Yes, I understand this has been said 20 or 40 times in earlier chapters. The fact is it needs repeating until exercise physiologists start listening.

> Why not fix your eyes on ASEP? Take the plunge and run the race that will set you free.

Presenting research at regional and national meetings defines the academic process, particularly the promotion in rank and tenure. The immediate problem is that the professors' pursuit of research does not help the students. While research is important, it is the responsibility of the college "teachers" to make sure the undergraduate degree is linked to financially sound career options. College students should graduate with a favorable opportunity of accessing a job that merits getting a college degree. Otherwise, going to college is a financial waste of time.

Students borrow large sums of money to attend college. Therefore, it is not surprising that students and their parents expect a credible job opportunity after graduation. And when it happens, everything is great. But, when it doesn't happen, which is 90% of the time, college graduates with the largest debt burden suffer in many ways, particularly a decrease in feelings of well-being.

> Believe what you hope for will happen by joining ASEP and growing beyond what you are today.

Strange as it sounds, college teachers seldom take the time to think about the fact that an academic degree without a credible career link often results in a long-term legacy of diminished health and self-esteem. That is why many exercise science college graduates find themselves saying, "Why did I even go to college? It was a waste of time and money." Instead of providing some assurance of things hoped for, students graduate with the feeling of being used and manipulated (5).

College teachers owe their best to the students. But, instead of working on behalf of their students, they allow them to wallow in mediocrity. It is not hard to understand why the professors try to escape their obvious faults by saying to the students, "When you graduate, you can complete an application to medical school or nursing?" This kind of thinking by the professors is their response to what they have grown accustomed to. Here again, the price of change is linked to the inertia of their doctorate experience and the students' poor education and meaningless jobs after college.

To add fuel to the students' disappointment and frustration, the professors' failure to grow beyond their feelings of not wanting to upset status quo is a price that is simply too high for the students. It is as though the faculty is afraid to take a chance for they are too uncomfortable with being different. You can almost hear them saying to themselves, "What if my tenured colleagues find out that I am thinking about being a member of ASEP and supporting Board Certification? It might influence whether I get tenure?" No one said that taking charge of your life is not without some battles and challenges. The price of change is often action that leads to reaction. However, whether it is favorable or unfavorable isn't really the point, but persistence at doing the right thing for the right reason is the point.

Theodore Roosevelt (6) said it best,

> It is not the critic who counts: not the man who points out how the strong man stumbled or where the doer of deeds could have done them better. The credit belongs to the man who is actually in the arena; whose face is marred by dust and sweat and blood; who strives valiantly; who errs, and comes short again and again, because there is no effort without error and shortcoming ....

If academic exercise physiologists would change how they think, they could change their future and that of their students. If that happened, the well-being of their students would be greatly improved. And yet, all it takes is one person with the desire to think as an ASEP exercise physiologist does. This means thinking about professionalism and the importance of a profession-specific organization versus a generic organization.

This thinking is no different from the present-day physical therapists who decided to become healthcare professionals on their terms. The ASEP leaders believe that we can do the same. All that is necessary is to follow the lead of the ASEP perspective regarding "who we are" and "what we do" (7). Our beliefs and thinking contribute to our decisions and behaviors and to our actions and our personality and character. The simple truth is that we can transcend our limits if we are willing to think as healthcare professionals all day long day-after-day.

Imagine the response of a large number of academic exercise physiologists who believe in the importance of professionalism in exercise physiology. Just imagine the influence of such thinking. Actually, that is exactly the significance of ASEP and the work of the leadership to promote the professionalization of exercise physiology. The truth is that everything they have been doing since 1997 has been consistent with the needed mental shift in "what is exercise physiology" and "who is an exercise physiologist" (7). The ASEP leaders understood 20+ years ago what business exercise physiologists are in. That is why they developed the first-ever exercise physiology code of ethics, academic accreditation, board certification, and professional practice documents (8–10). The concept of purpose and credibility was recognized, and it has been constantly articulated specifically on behalf of every exercise physiologist.

> Why not become an exercise physiology healthcare entrepreneur and take the business of exercise medicine healthcare into your own hands?

This focus on purpose and credibility applies to all exercise physiologists and not just the doctorate prepared exercise physiologists. This thinking is consistent with the vision and goals of other healthcare professions. Thus, it doesn't take a second breath to understand that what the present-day exercise physiology faculty is saying regarding exercise science is meaningless when it comes to locating a credible career in the public sector after graduation. The "red flags" are everywhere and they have been for decades. The ah-hah revelation is this: "Hello, wake up students and parents all across the United States."

We can transcend the limits of failed rhetoric by not spending thousands of dollars on degree programs that are not helpful when it comes to locating credible jobs after college? Academic exercise physiologists can do better at creating credible and ethical academic programs. After all, the purpose of earning a college degree is to increase the students' chances of living his or her dream of being successful. That is the bottom line.

If you are a college student or a parent with a son or daughter who is about to start college, take a minute to think about what Yogi Berra (11) said, "If you don't know where you're going, you're probably going to wind up someplace else." So, ask yourself these questions:

1. What do you want from going to college?
2. What do you really want to do with the short amount of time in college?
3. Do you want to be a personal trainer or an exercise physiologist?
4. Why not think outside the box and combine what has been done with what can still be done?

Take your time to think about these questions and let your thinking plant a seed in your mind. What do you want in life after college? What do you want to become as the outcome of paying for and earning a college degree? These questions should help you to work steadily towards becoming what you think about daily.

Remember that the first step to changing is the price of overcoming the force of inertia (i.e., status quo), which reminds me of what Andy van de Ven (12) said, "People resist change when it is not understood, is imposed, is perceived as threatening, has risks greater than its potential benefits or interferes with other priorities." Given that the ASEP leaders find it difficult to believe that academic exercise physiologists don't understand the reasons for changing from exercise science to exercise physiology (especially since ASEP cannot and would not impose or threaten change), they are confused when their colleagues say, "If it ain't broke, why fix it." Yet, clearly, the system is broken. There is a major problem with academia.

Transcending the Old Dogma

Most academic exercise physiologists consider their professional life as not being a big deal. They are very successful because they have a great job. They have an office space, a room and students to teach if they are interested, and they can spend most of the day in a laboratory observing their graduate students collecting data. They are not in the battle for the ownership of exercise physiology for many reasons. One reason is that their job is likely to be in the Department of Exercise Science or the Department of Kinesiology, or one of a dozen or more different departments.

Unless academic exercise physiologists reach out to ASEP for membership, they are predisposed to membership in the American College of Sports Medicine (ACSM) organization. While its title is "sports medicine," it integrates research in "exercise science and sports medicine." The word research is a big part of the old dogma that is considered to be the only way to securing a faculty position. Hence, more often than not, there is the perception of being part of a game with one set of rules, which are not designed to work on behalf of the students! Nothing is real or even important except publishing research.

However, this is just part of the problem. Until exercise physiologists stop waking up to constantly thinking about academic status and little else, the change process will be slow for a long time. It is that simple because unchallenged dogma will not change. But wake up they must if they are to experience the deep satisfaction that comes from helping their students be successful after college. Hence, nothing is important to us unless we make it important. Are your students and their successes important to you? That is the question, isn't it?

My point is this: While everyone spends many hours improving their work and relationships with friends, family, and colleagues, no one should make it all about themselves. Understandably, therefore, there are important rules of work and even passion for being a member of an organization. But, at the center of who we are and what we become as an individual and as an employee, we must not live to satisfy just our interests. We are also responsible for not allowing life's issues obscure our efforts in bringing happiness to others.

The very process of changing how we think is linked to the mental images that result from thinking beyond everyday pressures to stay the course. Otherwise there may be a point of no return! Hence, it becomes simple enough to say, "So be it and turn a deaf ear to the students' needs and request for discussions about career opportunities."

> When I think of the word bully, I am reminded that if your organization is being targeted, it is because the organization has something the bully wants.

Everyone understands that failure is part of the trying process. That is life. Why not go ahead a try and then try and try again? Yesterday's dogma of which many exercise physiologists are living today is not going to change without trying to change it. Yes, understandably, the fear of failure is keeping many exercise physiologists locked in the past. They are not only people who fear new ideas and the changing of their behavior, they are not leaders either.

Exercise physiologists must act as if they have already received, and that they are living the 21st century view of exercise physiology as a healthcare profession. They must understand that the founding of the American Society of Exercise Physiologists shows active faith, and that every thought of exercise physiologists as healthcare professionals is manifested through its vision.

Exercise physiologists can only be what they see themselves to be, and only attain what they believe themselves attaining. Isn't this the same with other professional organizations? They, too, have analyzed their situation and decided to become their vision. Exercise physiologists can do the same, and in fact that is exactly what the ASEP exercise physiologists have done. It takes great resolve to live according to what you think you are. The challenge in life is to nurture and express our unique skills and education.

Exercise physiologists must sustain the ASEP effort to reveal the gift of independence that makes all exercise physiologists the master of their future position in society. Academic exercise physiologists must act now to embrace ASEP and a better future for their students.

Vision, straight thinking, and action go together in sustaining the way to success. Yes, it is an effort of the will and there are many risks in life. But believe that every time a door shuts another door will open. So why not be positive, especially under the most challenging of times. Exercise medicine is the future of exercise physiology. It is the perfect outcome and self-expression financed by the non-healthy lifestyle of almost every human being on Earth.

Stop giving in to non-exercise physiologists and non-exercise physiology organizations. If you are a professor of exercise physiology, why not stop compromising the future of your students? Why not stop accepting yourself in the present-day circumstances of yesterday's thinking? Transcend such thinking by believing in yourself and others who live by their own standards and state of mind. These words are not written to make anyone unhappy, but rather to help all of us rise to the expectation of *who we are* and *what we do* as healthcare professionals.

Final Thoughts

None of what I have said is meant to hurt anyone's feelings. None of the words are used to minister to my pride for I am average at best. Nor am I interested in diminishing the glitter of other exercise physiologists or their crown of glory so common to academic thinking.

It is part of my purpose in life to be helpful and nothing more. Knowing that others may find this chapter interesting and/or helpful gives me contentment. And so, it is that when I think of tomorrow I am more hopeful of our decisions to bring victory to our students and the profession of exercise physiology. Please know that I fully understand that creative risk taking is always a problem for those who are determined to not give themselves the permission to be who they really are.

It follows that exercise physiologists must create lasting sustainability that positions the profession in line with its destiny. To be sure, a willingness to break with status quo is the only way to stop the continued takeover of exercise physiology by the generic organizations. The ASEP's leaders' ambitious and energetic expectations of an enduring profession are grounded in knowing who they are, what they care about, and what they love to do as professionals, and what they want to commit themselves to doing on behalf of the profession, students, and society.

Only 20 years in its founding, it is important to point out that ASEP's identity and purpose have not changed. The founders were unmistakably clear in their goals: **Exercise physiologists are healthcare professionals who need their own professional organization and everything that goes with the professionalization of exercise physiology**. Today, they are still doing what they said was the ASEP founding purpose. Neither the founders nor the organization have drifted from its core purpose and identity. Letting go of old ways, challenging old assumptions, and living in the present is the ASEP leaders' intention.

The fact that ASEP has consistently stayed true to its vision and mission speaks well for the Board of Directors and membership. In fact, it is sobering to look back across two decades of work and note the hard and difficult decisions made to keep ASEP on track with its organizational principles. Thanks goodness this has nothing to do with ego, but simply the understanding that is imperative to liberating exercise physiologists and their diverse talents pulling them into the future of what is exercise physiology.

References

1 Nightingale, E. (n.d.). AZ Quotes. (Online). www.azquotes.com/quote/519399.
2 American Society of Exercise Physiologists. (2016). Board Certified Exercise Physiologists: EPC Mission and Purpose. (Online). www.asep.org/index.php/epc-online/epc-missionpurpose/.
3 Boone, T. (2016). *ASEP's Exercise Medicine Text for Exercise Physiologists*. Beijing, China: Bentham Science Publishing.
4 DeVos, R. M. (n.d.). Good Reads. (Online). www.goodreads.com/quotes/102917-the-only-thing-that-stands-between-a-man-and-what.
5 Weissmann, J. (2013). Here's Exactly How Many College Graduates Live Back Home. The Atlantic. (Online). www.theatlantic.com/business/archive/2013/02/heres-exactly-how-many-college-graduates-live-back-at-home/273529/.
6 Roosevelt, T. (n.d.). (Online). www.inspirationpeak.com/cgi-bin/search.cgi?search= theodore+Roosevelt.
7 American Society of Exercise Physiologists. (2016). Definition of Exercise Physiology. (Online). www.asep.org/.
8 American Society of Exercise Physiologists. (2016). Standards of Professional Practice. (Online). www.asep.org/?q=services/standard.
9 American Society of Exercise Physiologists. (2016). Code of Ethics. (Online). www.asep.org/?q=organization/ethics.
10 American Society of Exercise Physiologists. (2016). Academic Accreditation. (Online). www.asep.org/?q=services/accreditation.
11 Berra, Y. (1989). *It Ain't Over….* New York: McGraw-Hill.
12 Van de Ven, A. (1989). Comments to the National Academy of Engineering/Commission on Behavioral and Social Science and Education Symposium. Designing for Technological Change: People in the Process. (Online). www.breakthroughthinking.pressbooks.com/chapter/the-people-involvement-phase/.
13 Shinn, F. S. (2013). *The Game of Life and How to Play It*. Mansfield Centre, CT: Martino Publishing.

12

TIME FOR A CHANGE

> The price of change requires your total commitment, mind and body. But then something great happens: True professionalism is lived, and now you are what you believed you were meant to be.

Ask the parents today, "What is the reason you sent your son or daughter to college?" Nine out of 10 times the parents will say, "We expected the college education to increase our son or daughter's chance of getting an excellent, high-paying job after college." That is what the college degree is all about, right? Not necessarily. The truth is your son's tuition debt paid the college teachers to do research while the adjuncts did the teaching.

It makes no sense that the faculty has not made it transparent whether this or that degree yields a great job opportunity or not. Many students graduate much worse off than they were before they started college. In fact, only a few colleges are willing to admit it. For example, the University of Louisiana in Lafayette, LA eliminated the philosophy major from its list of majors!

The idea that college is about promoting knowledge and developing students is good as long as the degree program yields positive career results. The more students think about their college experience in reference to their post-college career options the better the likelihood of experiencing success. For this reason, students need to know more about what it actually takes to be successful after college. In particular, they need to know the connection, if any, to different career opportunities and/or otherwise success in the workplace.

After all, it is obvious that the students, if not their parents, are responsible for paying back thousands of dollars in tuition and living expenses. The fact is many college graduates with a four-year degree are buried in their tuition debt. In 2008, 81% of adults thought college was a worthwhile investment. Just five years later, B. Berger (1) reported in the *U.S. News* that "… 57% think so." The ethical issue that is still not being addressed as it should be is the responsibility of the department chair, the faculty, and the administration who continue to offer the same academic degrees without any hope of the students finding credible work opportunities after college. It is past time for a change!

The Power of a Vision

To be sure, if everyone responsible for the quality of the students' education were honest about this topic, the whirlwind of despair would decrease. The process of changing would begin immediately with the ASEP vision to transform exercise science to exercise physiology.

Indeed, here is the reality, the dozens of off-shoots of the traditional physical education degree programs offered throughout the colleges and universities of the 21st century world of academia would be changed to exercise physiology to decrease the after college emotional trauma, depression, and despair. There are no real jobs in the public sector with an undergraduate degree in "sport science" or "kinesiology."

It is the truth. That is why ASEP is doing what it can to change these 20th century degree programs to exercise physiology. This is the reason why the organization was founded. Imagine the students that would be helped if the academic exercise physiologists would reach out to support ASEP. The secret isn't complicated. It begins with stepping in the direction you believe allows for success and there will be astounding results. Believe and it will become your reality. There is no reason to remain confined to our past.

It was the ASEP vision that inspired the first professional definitions of exercise physiology and exercise physiologists (2). As already stated several times earlier, the ASEP vision produced the first-ever exercise physiology code of ethics. Then, it inspired the first-ever development of the accreditation guidelines for Board Certified Exercise Physiologists, and the first-ever writing of the standards of professional practice for exercise physiologists. It was the vision of recognition as a healthcare profession that inspired the writing of the college text, *Introduction to Exercise Physiology* (3).

Solomon, the wise King of Israel stated in Proverbs 29:18 (NIV), "Where there is no revelation, people cast off restraint; but blessed is the one who heeds wisdom's instruction." Here, "revelation" is the same as "vision." Where there is no vision of exercise physiology as a healthcare profession (such as is the case with yesterday's thinking), there is no inspiration or wisdom to change. Also, without a vision, there is no reason to be optimistic. Unfortunately, the status quo of publishing research is believed to be good enough, which raises the question, "Is it enough?" The answer is "no" and so ASEP will not stop its work to expand the influence of exercise physiologists as healthcare entrepreneurs. Also, the ASEP members will not forget the importance of the ASEP vision and doing what they can to build the profession of exercise physiology.

The ASEP exercise physiologists see the future of exercise physiology and understand their destiny is healthcare. They believe that exercise physiologists can no longer turn a blind eye to the truth of what must be done to preserve the integrity of exercise physiology. Dr. Myles Munroe (4) said it best in his book, *The Principles and Power of Vision*, "Vision is seeing the future before it comes into being. It is a mental picture of your destiny."

The ASEP leaders' purpose is simple because they believe the destiny of exercise physiologists is healthcare, not athletics. They believe the ASEP vision gives purpose and meaning to exercise physiologists. They understand the academic exercise physiologists' role in publishing research is important, but real progress for all exercise physiologists is more than publishing another paper. Exercise physiology as a healthcare profession is more, and exercise physiologists who are willing to make the commitment to shared values can do significantly more as they learn to think differently and demonstrate the willingness to change.

The Exercise Physiologists' Purpose

If you are an exercise physiologist or plan to become one, do you have a sense of the "purpose" of exercise physiology? Do you know why exercise physiology exists? If you are a college professor doing research, you may say: "I believe the purpose of exercise physiology is to do research and publish scientific papers. The students getting a degree in exercise physiology are doing so because they are interested in nursing or physical therapy." What if they were not interested in either area of study, what then? The professor would probably say, "If you are referring to my undergraduates, then, I believe they should not get a major in exercise science, kinesiology, or a non-ASEP accredited exercise physiology degree because just about anyone can be a personal trainer."

Well, then, how do you feel about this statement:

> I think the undergraduate degree should be an ASEP accredited exercise physiology major. At graduation, the students should sit for the ASEP Board Certification. As a Board Certified Exercise Physiologist, they will earn the ASEP healthcare professional title that identifies then as being responsible for prescribing exercise medicine. In other words, the students graduate knowing who they are with their identity (i.e., their purpose).

Both accreditation and board certification are not play things in ASEP. They are more than a ploy to build membership. They are central to going forward to be true to who we are and have been since our core identity was defined in 1997. This is a pivotal point to emphasize, especially the fact that ASEP has a clear and compelling purpose of the future. This statement is no illusion. It is paved with difficult decisions that criticisms and/or challenges from individuals of generic organizations will not distract the leadership from their conviction to make the future a better place for the students of exercise physiology.

Meantime, it is depressing for college graduates without a meaningful job. There is the uncomfortable feeling of wasting one's potential as opposed to the feeling of growing and experiencing one's dreams. It is about asking what went wrong when life could have been different. Meanwhile, the professors still get their monthly paycheck to pay their bills and live comfortably. Lost in the noise of academic mediocrity they may wake up one day with questions from their sons and daughters. At first glance, they may be surprised but later they are likely to identify with the part they played. When you get a closer look, you will see that the faculty is lost in the midst of being ordinary.

I believe I was born to help with the development of exercise physiology as a healthcare profession and, in so doing, enable exercise physiologists to become leaders in prescribing exercise medicine to prevent and treat chronic diseases and disabilities. I have been writing and talking about the importance of exercise physiologists supporting ASEP and the vision of something better for all exercise physiologists for a long time. I will neither bury my dream nor struggle with self-doubt. I believe the dream of ASEP members is that exercise physiologists should be acknowledged as healthcare professionals. Singly and collectively, we have the enthusiasm and the drive to stay the course. Nobody will stop it from happening, regardless of the resistance, opposition, and challenges.

You may say, "Tommy, do you think your journal articles and books are going to make a difference?" My response should be obvious, "Yes, I do." It isn't the fact that I have three master's degrees above the Ph.D. degree or 44 years of college teaching, but rather my vision to live exercise physiology as a recognized and credible healthcare profession.

Ultimately, a gift such as I have described requires putting one's life into the work that must be done on a daily basis. There is no reason to acknowledge anyone who doesn't understand the ASEP vision (5). It is a waste of time since they have gone beyond the point of no return. What is important is to stop being controlled by the agenda of others, by looking ahead to the next generation of ASEP exercise physiologists who will help with the professionalization of exercise physiology, and by concentrating our time and commitment on the ASEP goals.

As ASEP certified healthcare professionals, we are educated and understand professional issues and concepts. Increasingly, we are becoming more proactive with a clear picture of our mission. We understand that mistakes will be made, but we are driven to keep on task regardless of the obstacles and challenges that will be addressed. We will never give up.

Final Thoughts

If you don't think something needs to change, go to the next sports medicine or exercise science meeting and look around. Ask yourself this question, "Why aren't the exercise physiologists recognized under their own professional organization?" The medical doctors have their own professional organization, which is true for all other healthcare professionals. Athletic training, strength and conditioning, physical therapist, nurses, and others have their own professional organization.

It is sad to see that exercise physiologists are still hanging with exercise science and, perhaps, worse than that, sports medicine. From the ASEP perspective, the reality is that the academic exercise physiologists continue to give away exercise physiology that helps to increase the security of the future of the generic organizations. Not only are the college students paying a heavy price, but so is exercise physiology.

But, remember this: As long as exercise physiologists hold on to the ASEP vision, there is always the hope and the expectation of moving forward. It is my expectation that exercise physiologists who are not part of ASEP will decide that they have had enough of being controlled by non-exercise physiologists. Such a decision should not only lead to increased self-confidence, it should also lead to supporting the ASEP professional infrastructure. Becoming an ASEP member and giving in to the building of our profession is the true beginning of something great.

It is distressing and unnerving that so few exercise physiologists have the guts to safeguard the vision and mission of ASEP. Yet, it is important to remember that Howard Marguleas said, "Never cease," which means never quit pursuing the opportunity to produce something different, such as ASEP. "Don't be satisfied" means stop with the status quo because it is an easy and safe way out. Show some backbone and stand up to the pressure to stay the same, and find a new reason to live and work, such as the hopes and dreams of better career opportunities for all ASEP members. Do this now not later, especially because it is contrary to status quo. Allow yourself the right and the time to think outside the box and remain mindful of the ASEP work to professionalize exercise physiology.

> *Key Point:* It is the responsibility of all exercise physiologists to remain faithful in doing what is necessary to safeguard the vision and mission of the ASEP organization. The place for all exercise physiologists is ASEP, regardless of the different battles raging in the different organizations to not lose the membership of hundreds if not thousands of exercise physiology members.

Why is ASEP the organization of exercise physiologists? The leaders believe in challenging the status quo and in thinking differently on behalf of all the exercise physiologists that have the right to their own professional organization. **How is ASEP going to compete with other organizations?** This is not a problem in the long run because ASEP is designed from the professional perspective that is no different from the other healthcare-specific organizations. The ASEP leadership understands the challenges and the battles that are expected, and they will deal with them as warriors of a new vision. **What is the significance of working to ensure the professionalism of all exercise physiologists?** It is the recognition of what is necessary to equip oneself with the prerequisites to achieve high quality professional success and respect of the medical community.

It all begins with ASEP and the "why statements" because it is logical, clear, and it makes sense. The ASEP vision is the path to success. It opens the door to what is necessary to define where exercise physiologists are going. Knowing "who you are" and "what you do" is a solid foundation from which organizational strength gives rise to purpose and possibilities. Grounded in why ASEP exist the members continue to speak to the core purpose that undergirds its vision. This is also why ASEP is the same today as it was in its beginning. It is hard to imagine today without ASEP and its influence on exercise physiology, which gives rise to great possibilities for all exercise physiologists.

References

1 Berger, B. (2013). Why a College Degree May Not Be Worth It. U.S. News. (Online). www.usnews.com/opinion/articles/2013/05/09/why-a-college-degree-no-longer-guarantees-success.
2 American Society of Exercise Physiologists. (2017). ASEP Home Page. (Online). www.asep.org/.
3 Boone, T. (2014). *Introduction to Exercise Physiology*. Burlington, NY: Jones and Bartlett Publishing.
4 Munroe, M. (2003). *The Principles and Power of Vision*. New Kensington, PA: Whitaker House.
5 American Society of Exercise Physiologists. (2017). ASEP Vision. (Online). www.asep.org/.

13
EXERCISE PHYSIOLOGY AND BUSINESS

While there are problems that need correcting in academic exercise physiology, particularly with regard to career opportunities for the students of exercise physiology, the lack of the students' education in business is also problematic. The students receive no training in entrepreneurship and business management. The lack of business courses in the exercise physiology curriculum is not a new problem. Students graduate without understanding the steps necessary to start their own exercise medicine business.

> The price of change requires commitment.

Without the necessary education, it is too late to do well at transitioning from college to the work environment. That is part of the reasons why young adults find themselves out of a job and back home with their parents. Obviously, such an outcome is not what the parents want and, frankly, a steady job is an important means to paying back student loans and getting on with life. The students' post-college reality is related to the failure of the department, faculty, and degree program that do not require: (a) training in professional networks; (b) availability of financing and capital; (c) location of a business; (d) amount of time and effort involved; (e) willingness to take risks; and (f) business management skills to build an exercise medicine healthcare business.

On the other hand, if the exercise physiology college graduates were prepared to manage the business aspects of an exercise medicine practice, life after college would be much better. This is an important point, given today's emphasis on the prevention and treatment of non-communicable diseases with exercise medicine. Imagine students with both the knowledge of how to safely prescribe exercise medicine and the business knowledge to successfully build their own healthcare practice (1). This outcome would prove to be a critical step in the right direction for all the obvious reasons. For certain, there would be the realization that the students' college education is actually paying off and, thus "getting a college degree" would be viewed as being worth both the time and financial investment.

The Disconnect

The failure of academic exercise physiologists to connect with the business world and healthcare services is evident throughout the degree programs. The problem is twofold. First, there is the obvious stumbling block that exercise physiologists think of themselves as researchers and not as healthcare professionals. Second, academic exercise physiologists do not think as healthcare entrepreneurs, which is a problem.

The key issue is not complicated. The professors are not focusing on the students and their career needs. The department is not doing its best to prepare the students for work after college. This should sound the alarm for institutions that desire to remain true to their mission.

> If exercise physiologists have not agreed as to what needs to be taught, they cannot expect college graduates to possess such knowledge outside of what has been required of them in the curriculum. If business is believed to be important, then it is important that faculty members re-examine what they are teaching to exercise physiology students.

While it is important that students take exercise physiology courses and participate in the hands-on laboratory sessions, both are insufficient in meeting the students' needs after college. Students should also take business courses to learn how to start a healthcare business. Then, the students will be prepared to applied exercise medicine within their own healthcare clinic.

If knowing how to start and operate an exercise medicine healthcare clinic is critical to the success of students after college, why can't the academic exercise physiologists update the exercise physiology curriculum to include two or three business courses? Why can't they be more like the academic physical therapists who do an excellent job of helping their students integrate standards of practice and business management skills with their patients after surgery and during the treatment of musculoskeletal disorders in their own clinics?

College professors faced with the decision as to whether they should spend more time doing research or helping their students, the ASEP leaders would say spend more time with your students. The leaders understand that research is the "academic game," but why compromise the academic mission when the lack of student success after college decreases the value of a college degree and exercise physiology.

After all, the students' education should be more about what will help to ensure career success that promotes the profession of exercise physiology.

Understanding Business Issues

It is the responsibility of the exercise physiology faculty, the department chair, and the college administration to initiate change in the curriculum to help ensure the students' success after college. Exercise physiology students must be taught how to write a business plan for their practice of exercise medicine. They need an understanding of the business issues, especially how much clients are willing to pay, how payment for services will be made (such as out-of-pocket), and the specifics of a financial plan to start a healthcare practice.

> I knew that whoever embraced professionalism and business management held the power. It was the key to their success and credibility

At the heart of the exercise physiology degree is its teachers. The teachers are providers of care for students. They are critical to the credibility of the teaching process and the profession. Hence, the growth of exercise physiology is dependent on the integrity of the college teachers. They are responsible for ensuring that business concepts are part of the students' academic course work. But, unfortunately, until the college teachers understand the importance of thinking differently, their self-centeredness will delay the transformation required to overcome the 20th century dogma.

As Ruth Callanta noted, "We are too self-centered, too selfish to be able to make a difference in the lives of other people." As I read her comment, the point that got my attention was its similarity to organizations that are driven by power, politics, and greed. It is inconceivable that in the foreseeable future students will have the opportunity to get an ASEP accredited exercise physiology degree with a minor in business without a change the hearts of the professors. Not until they recognize their self-centeredness will the college graduates have the scientific and business education for success as healthcare entrepreneurs.

Another critically important academic adjustment within the future doctorate programs will be either the combined Doctor of Philosophy (Ph.D.) and Master of Business Administration (MBA) degree or the Ph.D. in exercise physiology with a minor in business administration. The rationale for this thinking is simply that the faculty is expected to promote exercise physiology, business management, and entrepreneurship. The faculty is also expected to join and support the American Society of Exercise Physiologists and its work in promoting professionalism in exercise physiology.

Faculty advisors will help students who are majoring in exercise physiology to understand that it is necessary to be willing to take risks when it comes to starting their own businesses. Entrepreneurship is for students who are determined and optimistic, and who want to make a difference in the lives of their future clients and/or patients. The time and effort required to raise capital and/or use their personal savings bear directly on the success of starting a business. They should also know that it is important to abide in Christ and make a commitment to integrity as an exercise medicine healthcare provider.

For these reasons and others (such as understanding the healthcare industry, ethical issues, networking, regulations, taxes, and costs of employee benefits), it is clear that exercise physiologists as college teachers also need an understanding of professionalism and fundamentals of business and management to help with their students' future well-being. Otherwise, it is inexcusable to protect one's own career by advising a senior to complete an application to graduate school because the professor has done nothing to promote exercise physiology as a healthcare profession.

Academic exercise physiologists can do much better as college teachers by listening to their students, especially the recent graduates. They can help by demonstrating the willingness to learn, adapt, and change from thinking just about research to "research, teaching, students, healthcare, and entrepreneurship." In short, their ability to communicate and market exercise physiology as a healthcare profession is no different from the students' responsibility to do the same when they graduate from college. If the teachers do it, the students will be successful. If they don't, the lack of foundational competencies necessary to effectively do something about teaching and entrepreneurial thinking will continue to act as a major barrier to the students' success.

Students need to know up front that an exercise physiology practice is stressful and risky. This is true even when working with someone else, such as a partner who may increase the success of the business. There may be differences of opinion. Thus, not surprisingly, going solo is likely to be the major choice by many exercise physiologists, especially given the freedom to make their own business decisions and get all the profits. The following questions will help answer whether going solo or having a partner is the right path for you:

1. Do you prefer working on your own or with another person?
2. Do you prefer working out solutions to problems by yourself or with another person?
3. Are you confident in creating, growing, and answering questions and concerns about the business (e.g., how to start it, how to keep it going, and how to increase revenue) or would you prefer working with someone else and look to him or her to make suggestions?

There are numerous other points of interest, particularly with regard to providing services to clients at a specific, agreed upon rate driven by a cash-based exercise physiology healthcare practice. The advantage of an out-of-pocket cash-based practice is that the owner does not have to work with insurance companies at an agreed upon reimbursement rate. The cash-based practice is also less paperwork and hassle.

Second, there is the concern regarding the location of the exercise medicine business and whether it will have a positive or a negative influence on the clients. Third, the exercise physiologist as an entrepreneur must understand the tax implications and fees for small businesses in his or her state, city, and county. Fourth, regarding referral providers (such as medical doctors), do they know what Board Certified Exercise Physiologist do? Are they willing to refer their patients to an exercise medicine clinic? Are there other exercise physiologists working in the same area? Fifth, is the exercise medicine clinic accessible to clients and patients? How will they know where it is located? Is the signage visible (1)?

Students also need information regarding what type of exercise physiology practice they are most interested in (e.g., children, teenagers, athletes, or adults)? How will the clients help build a successful exercise medicine practice? What is the market potential? What kind of equipment is needed to help the clients get better? What is the best strategy for staying positive, energetic, and motivated while working towards short-term and long-term goals relative to sales, financing, and hiring along with staying on top of your business goals and objectives. Is your business plan completed (1)? What will be the anticipated income in one year and two years? What is expected to happen if the market share renders less revenue than required to financially survive? What about legal advice and/or professional guidance?

Final Thoughts

Appropriately 82% of adults have at least one risk factor for heart disease (4). Hence, why not help students to think about what type of exercise physiology practice is interesting to them? Exercise medicine can increase the quality of life of Americans by preventing and reducing the negative effects of cardiovascular (heart) disease, mental depression, type 2 diabetes, hypertension, cancer, high cholesterol, and obesity.

> The importance of "what we think" seems so clear, but do we actually believe it. I know it matters just as "what we talk about" drives what we do or will do. Remember, if we think we can or can't we are right.

Society needs more ASEP Board Certified Exercise Physiologists. Why? Because 65% of American adults are overweight, 31% of American adults are obese (5), approximately 105 million American adults have high cholesterol (defined as 200 mg·dL^{-1} or higher) (6), approximately 50 million Americans have hypertension (7), approximately 30 million Americans have heart disease (8), and at least 16 million Americans have diabetes (8).

Campbell and Campbell (9) said, "Never before have such large percentages of the population died from diseases of affluence." It is interesting that while the public is just beginning to understand the power of regular exercise to prevent chronic diseases, the majority of the population is still not interested in doing the work that is necessary to improve their lifestyle for better health and well-being.

Equally interesting is the problem of many academic exercise physiologists who continue to turn a deaf ear to ASEP, which is their healthcare organization. Given that exercise medicine can prevent and treatment chronic diseases and disabilities of the mind and body (10), promoting both ASEP and Board Certified Exercise Physiologists would increase the population's health, well-being, and longevity (11).

The problem with academic exercise physiologists starts with their doctorate education. Unfortunately, the overwhelming emphasis on research at the expense of teaching is bad for students. The correction to this problem starts with exercise physiologists' recognition they are hooked on an outdated system of education. Academic exercise physiologists simply cannot let the status quo go unchallenged and watch our young adults continue to suffer. It is time to stand up and take control of the profession of exercise physiology and dare to make a difference in the face of indifference.

References

1 Boone, T. (2012). *The Business of Exercise Physiology*. Lewiston, NY: The Edwin Mellen Press.
2 Wadhwa, V., Aggarwal, R., Holly, K. Z., & Salkever, A. (2009). The Anatomy of an Entrepreneur: Making of a Successful Entrepreneur. Kauffman: The Foundation of Entrepreneurship. (Online). www.kauffman.org/what-we-do/research/2010/05/the-anatomy-of-an-entrepreneur.
3 Stafford, T. (2009). More Than Profit: A Business Plan with a Divine Edge Has an Angle on Fighting Poverty. Christianity Today. (Online). www.christianitytoday.com/ct/2009/september/31.70.html.
4 Centers for Disease Control and Prevent. (2011). Prevalence of Coronary Heart Disease: United States 2006–2010. (Online). www.cdc.gov/mmwr/preview/mmwrhtml/mm6040a1.htm.
5 Flegal, K. M., Carroll, M. D., Ogden, C. L., et al. (2002). Prevalence and Trends in Obesity among U.S. Adults. 1999–2000. *Journal of American Medical Association*. 288: 1723–1727.
6 American Heart Association. (2014). High Blood Cholesterol and Other Lipids—Statistics. (Online). www.americanheart.org/presenter.Jhtml?Identifier=2016.
7 Wolf, M., Cutler, J., Roccella, E. J., et al. (2000). Statement from the National High Blood Education Program: Prevalence of Hypertension. *American Journal of Hypertension*. 13: 103–104.
8 Lucas, J. W., Schiller, J. S., & Benson, V. (2004). National Center for Health Statistics. *Vital Health Statistics*. 10: 218.
9 Campbell, T. C., & Campbell, T. M. (2006). *The China Study*. Dallas, TX: BenBella Books.
10 Booth, F. W., Roberts, C. K., & Laye, M. J. (2012). Lack of Exercise Is a Major Cause of Chronic Diseases. *Comparative Physiology*. 2: 1143–1211.
11 Boone, T. (2016). Board Certified Exercise Physiologists and Exercise Medicine: A 2016 Perspective. *Journal of Exercise Medicine*. 1, 2: 1–25.

14

THE ASEP PATH

Yes, I understand the future is not an easy place to make changes. Written across the pages of the past 20 years of ASEP, the academic exercise physiologists have failed to challenge exercise science and sports medicine. It is disappointing, and it is seriously disturbing. As I have pointed out many times, ASEP exercise physiologists understand exercise science and similar academic degree titles are not exercise physiology. They understand that surrendering to the irrational belief system that is allowing the failed rhetoric to remain unchanged is the easy way out.

Academic exercise physiologists sit at the feet of tradition in academia, which is publishing research that gives them the freedom to think in accordance with their needs. They are rewarded with big money doing research while staying out of the classroom. After all, it is clear that a professor's reputation is built through research and not teaching.

As chance would have it while teaching in six colleges and universities, I was involved in numerous discussions with other faculty members about teaching. It was clear that the majority of the academic exercise physiologists drifted from one course to the next as though the classroom was "dead time." Teaching had become nothing more than a requirement of the academic bureaucracy. It was a no-brainer that the research culture is a powerful force to deal with.

Change is not only inevitable, it is imperative. This point is clarified by Bill Phillips and Michael D'Orso in their book, *Body for Life* (1), "Once the truth is revealed, the path becomes clear." The truth is apathy towards college teaching. This truth is a huge danger to our students. Students must be engaged by teachers who love to teach, who are not restricted by the research dogma, and who are willing to bring something original and unique into teaching. Hence, if the academic degree is meant to be meaningful, then teaching must be valued by the academic administration. The faculty must take responsibility as "teachers" to emphasize the importance of teaching and its role in opening up the world of healthcare and common sense thinking.

> **Key Point**: If we believe in the values inherent in the teaching process and if we believe that the practice of exercise medicine requires knowledgeable healthcare professionals, then we must get to work and do all we can to promote college excellence in teaching.

Today, *exercise is scientifically recognized as medicine*, and it should be prescribed by academically qualified healthcare providers. Therefore, the ASEP preoccupation with the college teachers' passion for teaching intentionally sends the message that the students' career success is more important than the teachers' research publications. **With this in mind, exercise is the 21st century medicine that college graduates who are ASEP Board Certified Exercise Physiologists will use to make their success happen**. Here is where we overcome our limiting beliefs.

Naturally, it is worth mentioning and celebrating the work of the department chair and faculty who earned the title "ASEP Accredited Exercise Physiology Program" from which the students qualify to sit for the ASEP Board Certification (EPC) exam to produce the new generation of exercise physiologists (2). This awareness of the importance of a profession-specific accreditation has never been lost by the ASEP leaders.

Just as with other healthcare professionals, ASEP exercise physiologists cannot expect clients to simply accept on blind faith that they know what they are doing. Rather, the underlying message of knowing who you are, what you love, what you are qualified to do, and what you are willing to do to commit your life to helping clients is fulfilling your purpose.

While licensure is important from several different perspectives, it is not mandated as a requirement for healthcare professionals. The professionalization process of all professions is always ongoing (3). Acknowledging this point earlier on, the ASEP leaders felt that it was (and still is) the right step to take in creating the profession-specific Board Certification for exercise physiologists. This was done to unify the profession. Unity is the central characteristic of a profession, and it is this unity that will compel others to pay attention to the ASEP message and vision. It was also done to promote their identity as healthcare providers.

Speaking with a Single Voice

It shouldn't come as a surprise that the ASEP members have been confronted by colleagues who disagree with the ASEP initiatives regarding exercise physiology.

Why, because the ASEP organization is doing what it can to change the exercise science title to exercise physiology (i.e., if the exercise science curriculum is updated and the program meets ASEP standards). Aside from the academic exercise physiologists who are slow to change their thinking, there are also college teachers who have a doctorate degree in sports science, human performance, kinesiology, and similar degree programs who are simply not interested in speaking with a single voice.

> There is an expression "why fix it, if it ain't broke" but this is not true. Students graduate from exercise science and related degree programs, including exercise physiology due to the status quo mentality of the academic exercise physiologists, without finding credible career opportunities.

And yet, until we and our colleagues agree that change is necessary to benefit the students, they will remain divided by titles and diminished by the lack of desire and willingness to support new ideas. It is frustrating and a sad state of affairs the faculty find themselves in since physical therapists, athletic trainers, physician assistants, social workers, nurses, and occupation therapists understand the necessity of supporting their own professional-specific organization (4). Yes, other healthcare professionals have professional issues and concerns as well but at least they are willing to find creative solutions.

Now that aerobic exercise and anaerobic exercise are recognized as medicine to prevent and/or treat individuals with cardiovascular diseases, hypertension, obesity, type 2 diabetes mellitus, depression, and some forms of cancer (5), the exercise physiology students have a fantastic opportunity to create their own exercise medicine clinics. This is especially the case when students graduate from an ASEP accredited institution and pass the ASEP Board Certification exam to earn the professional title, ASEP Board Certified Exercise Physiologist. Both the ASEP certification and the ASEP academic accreditation guidelines are responsible for helping to promote the first-ever exercise physiology professional standards and practices (6).

For the person who has not considered these comments before now, my point is that we are authors of our own future. The most successful professionals "walk their talk." However, if academic exercise physiologists, in particular, continue to acquiesce to the academic 20th-century thinking, there is the increased likelihood that the profession of exercise physiology will not grow in maturity until many decades later. The emphasis on research will continue to dominate exercise physiology. Thus, it should then be obvious that only the academic exercise physiologists will survive. No one else will. Forget about the students who graduate with a major in exercise physiology. Either they will apply to graduate school or go back home to live.

> The ASEP exercise physiologists are building a new exercise physiology profession.

However, if we come together as a united force to grow exercise physiology, our unique strengths will prevail. Then, as a united professional force, our students will benefit from the ASEP accredited exercise physiology curriculum that drives the career-specific exercise medicine options. The exercise physiology students will also have a much better idea of who is suited to receive their services. They will know how to provide exercise medicine and why their services are different from non-exercise physiology services. Their teachers will have provided them critical information about how to write a business plan, create a marketing strategy to help establish a business budget, get the exercise medicine services up and running, develop a positive and ethical rapport with clients and patients, and how to safely prescribe exercise medicine to different ages and gender.

ASEP Organization and Possibilities

Credibility is not negotiable. Propelled by faith, the ASEP leaders understand the link between professionalism and exercise physiology services. Their focus is on a higher level of servant leadership and less on self-serving goals. As time has passed since the first ASEP national meeting, the leadership has committed itself to an increasingly higher academic standard. The organization is dedicated to maintaining the highest levels of quality for all ASEP Board Certified Exercise Physiologists.

> A college faculty job is really a research position that is indicative of the academic culture based on self-centered values of the institution's thinking.

The ASEP paradigm, however unlikely that it still exists today is nonetheless secure in its vision and goals. It is a small organization, but its members understand the need to focus on professionalism and purposeful change. The leadership is trustworthy, honest, and truthful with the members. They believe exercise physiology is too important to settle for mediocrity. Therefore, their thoughts and work have created a new culture of exercise physiologists who are not afraid to challenge old assumptions and find new solutions. They get that ASEP is big in dreams when it gives rise to the right attitude. As Winston Churchill, the British statesperson and U.K. Prime Minister said, "Attitude is a little thing that makes a big difference."

All professions need visionaries and their work to nurture unity, growth, and professional development of its members. Small things matter, such as the act of celebrating ASEP. It is a major transformation and a major step forward that constantly touches the heart of **what is exercise physiology** and **who is an exercise physiologist**. I am convinced that the ASEP organization is needed to deal with the politics of academia, the semantic impasses, and the specialized ideologies that are so evident at all levels in academia and among many exercise physiologists.

While it is obvious that the commitment to ASEP is confusing to members of the giant generic organizations, others find themselves staring at the opportunity to make a difference but are too uncomfortable and scare to take the risk. As Dennis told Joey in a Dennis the Menace cartoon, "You can't live in the past. That was this *morning!*" The world is changing. Exercise physiologists must take advantage of the "exercise medicine" opportunity and align themselves with the ASEP healthcare purpose and vision.

Regular exercise empowers the mind and body by producing positive health benefits. The practical inroad to professional recognition will be healthcare in addition to research and athletic performance. A more health-conscious society will no doubt align itself with Board Certified Exercise Physiologists. There will be major changes in the academic curriculum. The exercise physiology degree and the generic degree titles will be updated. ASEP accreditation will focus more on the prevention of health issues and less on research to empower the exercise physiology students and to create the profound link between college and career opportunities.

The framework of our healthcare practice will reflect the need to learn more about entrepreneurship, business mechanics, and professional relationships with the medical community. Board Certified Exercise Physiologists will be better prepared to evaluate their clients and embrace possibilities of better health, manage their clients' stress and anxiety levels, offer mutually supportive advice, and provide productive ways to promote the clients' mind-body health and well-being.

The great challenge for the ASEP leaders is to continue moving in an elaborate and diverse means of providing healthcare ideas, commitment, and concepts for building a healthier tomorrow. They will help exercise physiologists learn the importance of taking risks to help create a healthcare environment that will give profound meaning to their clients' health and wellness. After all, it is their intention and willingness as exercise medicine healthcare professionals to bring meaning to the exercise medicine experience.

Accountability Is Imperative

The academic institutions, departments, and faculty must be held accountable to providing an education that is career-specific. It is that simple, and I believe it is just a matter of time before society demands it. Otherwise, if the change process is prolonged, present-day families should avoid sending their children to college. Why, because there is a profound interconnection between the purpose-driven degree and dramatic success after college. If the academic setting is linked to the uniqueness of co-creating career opportunities, then all is well. The intent and mission of the degree and the faculty are student-centered.

While it is easy to leave the administration and the faculty unchecked, it is wrong for many reasons. Accountability is the right course of action, and there isn't any question that the exercise science and similar degrees should be updated in accordance with ASEP accreditation guidelines. The faculty should be held to a higher ethical and academic standard. Student (and their parents) deserve the most effective and efficient education possible.

Hence, it is imperative that all academic exercise physiologists share in the ASEP power of dreams and the potential for greatness as a healthcare profession. It is the dream of something better for everyone interested in transcending the old to make a difference in the students' lives. From deep within each of us is the great desire to promote who we are, what we do, and why we are prepared and will not fail as credible healthcare professionals. As Malcolm X said, "Tomorrow belongs only to the people who prepare for it today."

With that said, each of us needs to get rid of the old ways of thinking. Yesterday's physical education's transition to kinesiology or exercise science or even human performance is done. It is time to move on, and it is time to act now. And yes, it requires acting to move away from the tyranny of the past, which will happen only when exercise physiologists allow themselves to embrace the ASEP future.

The **Establishment** will not help our students or the profession of exercise physiology. Once again, it *requires action* to experience change and to embrace the vitality of the future. With more diligence we put into moving on, and with the right reflection, drive, and honesty, we will become our dream. Now, open up your mind to the future expectation of all exercise physiologists graduating from an ASEP accredited institution with a degree in exercise physiology.

Fortunately, the emphasis on exercise medicine to prevent and treat chronic diseases is here to stay as middle-aged and older Americans realize their relationship to healthcare issues. ASEP Board Certified Exercise Physiologists are building relationships, particularly with the medical community. In time, they will be recognized as one of the pillars by which society will become safely transformed to a healthier lifestyle. This new paradigm is expected even though exercise physiologists do not have a shared access and usage of healthcare reimbursement. However, until present-day licensure becomes reality, if that is determined to be a necessary factor for success, client payment for services rendered by Board Certified Exercise Physiologists will provide a significant financial income.

What the future holds for the exercise physiology profession is also related to the decreased mediocrity or the old paradigm common to exercise science. It is as Ronald Reagan said, "Status quo is, you know, Latin for the 'The mess we're in.'" The ASEP leaders understand the attitude of the politically-driven organizations as well as the faculty members being comfortable with the Establishment. They understand the uncomfortable feelings and insecurity of being told that accountability is not just important but imperative. They know there are opposing forces to ASEP, but they also know that learning and improving together as agents of change are all driven by the desire to live exercise physiology as a healthcare profession.

The ASEP leaders let go of status quo years prior to the 1997 founding of the "Society" of exercise physiologists. They knew that leaders are future-focused with the courage, conviction, and drive to challenge the old paradigm because their planning of a better future for the "students of exercise physiology" requires them to look forward and create a better exercise physiology with new and young healthcare professionals (7).

Accountability is about being a good and competent exercise physiologist who is supportive and ethical either as a teacher or a practicing healthcare professional. It is the sharing of the heart's way of becoming something more, which is exactly what a vision is about. Rosabeth Moss Kanter, a professor at Harvard Business School said it this way, "A vision is not a picture of what could be; it is an appeal to our better selves, a call to become something more."

No Excuses!

It is not enough to want to be a gymnast. It must also be a calling to become a gymnast. Then, you must have the guts to become a gymnast (8). No doubt the fear of getting hurt keeps many from trying. But, rather than admitting it, all you hear is excuse after excuse. No one is going to become a gymnast without moving beyond their comfort zone and yet, the idea of becoming an athlete can be a calling to become something more.

But, then, just a few feet away from the parallel bars is the high bar! Do you risk falling? No one wants to get hurt, but learning a new sport or a combination of skills in the rings requires trying? A person cannot become a gymnast if he or she is not willing to take ownership of the learning process. In other words, learning a new way to think is *the power within* you to try (9). It is also the responsibility that a person accepts while acknowledging the risks. Being an athlete is like being an ASEP member. Both start with the desire from within you. How will you change, adapt, and evolve over time without the desire to do so?

Similarly, the work of the ASEP organization takes commitment. There is always the concern: "What will I lose? How will it hurt me? Will it hurt someone I care about?" The bottom line is that change begins with becoming a warrior for something different even though the supporters of the Establishment will question your credibility by suggesting that you did this or that when none of it is true. Also, if they think you are successful in getting others to support the change process, they will try to remove you from your position of influence. They will share lies with others that there must be something wrong with you. They may even say you should be terminated from your job. If that doesn't work, they will do just about anything to isolate you and marginalize you and your thinking.

While the behavior of status quo supporters is often questionable if not unethical and hurtful, their behavior is driven by their fear of being inadequate (much like the would-be gymnast who is too scared to try). Their resistance lies within themselves. Their way of making the world a better place to live is to steal from the accomplished work of others.

Creating the future isn't easy. You can't please everyone, and that is not an excuse. It is simply the truth. So, please remember when the behavior of your colleagues is wrong, and everyone knows it even though they are not interested in pointing it out for fear of what might happen to them, forgive your colleagues anyway. Think healthy thoughts and keep at the change process. New thoughts and beliefs are critical to a lasting and significant change. For after all, we become what we think, so choose your thoughts carefully, especially the thinking that can be consciously helpful to ourselves and others (10).

> ***Where to from Here?*** The absence of bold and authentic leadership in exercise physiology is a tragedy. Exercise physiologists have so much to offer to society in the name of exercise medicine. But, the students are not taught the actual application in society, only the steps necessary to past an exam. ***They know little to nothing about how to start a business, such as an Exercise Medicine Clinic or how to think as an entrepreneur.*** The effects of not receiving a credible education are far reaching (11).

Final Thoughts

As strange as it seems, the future is now for everyone who is living their dream. Keep in mind that the ASEP reality is not as big as organizations that have been around for 50 or 100 years. But it does exist, and it is representative of the new generation of exercise physiologists. It is the product of measurable outcomes that are attainable, relevant, and key to the students' growth in the exercise physiology profession.

There isn't any question that the new generation of exercise physiologists will carry the message forward. They will be responsible for communicating the ASEP vision, for clarifying why the ASEP goals and objectives are important, and for helping to share the message of empathy and hope. They will understand the necessity of not doing what their friends and colleagues have always done. They understand the change they desire for themselves and their colleagues, and they are willing to stand up and make a difference.

The ASEP members and Board Certified Exercise Physiologists will be the new generation of exercise physiologists. They will individually and collectively be recognized as the future of exercise physiology with the education to make a difference in society's healthcare needs as exercise medicine professionals. With this in mind, in a sincere and genuine way, why not ask yourself, "Isn't it time that academic exercise physiologists admit their mistakes, regardless of how it may make them feel and open up the future to unlimited possibilities for our students?" The answer is "Yes," and the reason is because it is the best decision to make in that it underscores the academic exercise physiologists' integrity and courage to do the right thing for the right reason for both the profession and the students of exercise physiology.

While the Establishment is always going to persist with the inevitable question, "Why waste your time?" Remember, every decision and action that the ASEP leaders take is for the purpose of influencing and motivating every exercise physiologists to embrace and support the ASEP vision. Every ASEP member deserves the comment, "You are a winner! You have overcome the fear of falling or getting hurt, which means you are well on your way to being a leader in the exercise physiology profession. Congratulations."

References

1 Phillips, B., & D'Orso, M. (1999). *Body for Life: 12 Weeks to Mental and Physical Strength*. New York: Harper Collins.
2 Boone, T. (2015). *Promoting Professionalism in Exercise Physiology*. Lewiston, NY: The Edwin Mellen Press.
3 Boone, T. (2009). *The Professionalization of Exercise Physiology: Certification, accreditation, and standards of practice of the American Society of Exercise Physiologists (ASEP)*. Lewiston, NY: The Edwin Mellen Press.
4 Boone, T. (2014). *Introduction to Exercise Physiology*. Burlington, MA: Jones and Bartlett Learning.
5 Boone, T. (2016). *ASEP's Exercise Medicine Text for Exercise Physiologists*. Beijing, China: Bentham Science Publishing.
6 Boone, T. (2001). *Professional Development of Exercise Physiology*. Lewiston, NY: The Edwin Mellen Press.
7 Smith, A. (1975). *Powers of Mind*. New York: Random House.
8 Boone, T. (1979). *Better Gymnastics: How to spot the performer*. Mountain View, CA: World Publications.
9 Boone, T. (2002). *The Power Within: The integration of faith and purposeful self-care in the 21st century*. Blomington, IN: AuthorHouse.
10 Boone, T., & Boone, E. (2018). *The Life Changing Power of The Lord's Prayer*. Bloomington, IN: WestBow Press.
11 Boone, T. (2012). *The Business of Exercise Physiology*. Lewiston, NY: The Edwin Mellen Press.

EPILOGUE

> He who does not know professionalism cannot understand the disorder of exercise physiology.

The past several years has been tough, hard, and interesting. Although it is strange to say it, college teachers don't care much about teaching and, frankly, will do just about anything to get out of doing so. The shocking truth is that none of this is covered-up. It is just the way it is in the academic setting.

The absence of bold and authentic leadership among academic exercise physiologists is tragic and shocking. The exercise physiologists have so much to offer to society in the name of exercise medicine (1). But, even though the students are spending $25,000 to $50,000 or more a year for at least four years to earn a degree that does not guarantee a financially decent job, they are not taught the actual application of exercise medicine in society. They know relatively little to nothing about how to start a business, such as an Exercise Medicine Clinic or how to think as an entrepreneur, which is most unfortunate.

The fact that academic institutions do not prepare students for jobs is a major concern. In fact, it is scary to think about. Yet, the reality of academia is the outcome of not receiving a credible education, which results more often than not in a night shift job at the local Starbucks (2). And yet, the question remains: Why is it that academia does not prepare students to be more entrepreneurial? Why isn't the institution, from the President to the department faculty members, held accountable for teaching students how to be healthcare professionals and how to start an exercise medicine clinic?

The moral of the story is that academic departments and degree programs are not always what they appear to be. That is why it is time for a serious reality check.

What is wrong? The problem is that academic exercise physiologists are not looking beyond their research. What is needed is a fundamental shift in thinking about why the students go to college. Getting a college degree just to be told to get another degree is not the answer to the problems that meaningless college degrees create, which raises the question: How is it that physical therapists do research and teach about ethics, professionalism, and standards of professional practice while academic exercise physiologists don't? The short answer is this: Physical therapists are members of their own professional organization that hold them accountable to adhering to the ethical standards of physical therapy and the principles of professionalism.

Exercise physiologists have been on their knees so long as supporters of sports medicine and exercise science that it seems impossible for them to get up. Only a handful of brave souls have managed to do so. Why? Because they felt that it was the right thing to do. They opened their eyes and hearts and they felt the true reality of the sports medicine and exercise science Establishment and its negative effects on the students and their families.

They understand that the job market for ASEP college students in exercise physiology is good and getting better due to the ASEP 21st century emphasis on Exercise Medicine (1). It is the means to parting with the past, and it is "the foundation" from which ASEP exercise physiologists are building the profession of exercise physiology. Hence, it is "the beginning point" that students will actually have the opportunity to be financially successful without spending more tuition dollars on another degree.

Think about it: The contribution of exercise medicine is the new and better paradigm, but the business venture must be spearheaded by leaders who get it. The ASEP leaders understand what is necessary to move forward to educate the students and provide them with the hope and expectation of transformational success. They understand that it is going to require hard work and dedication to make the ASEP exercise physiologists the new and successful healthcare career paradigm (3).

The ASEP exercise physiologists are gifted with the desire to grow and express themselves. Hence, it is reasonable to believe they will continue to help the academic exercise physiologists get the message that their job isn't just about them but more about their students. Imagine the impact if they were to think beyond themselves to help their students try new and creative ideas to increase career opportunities. Their reality is defined by how the college professors choose to connect and relate to them.

The re-organization of exercise physiology sets the stage for shattering the status quo paradigm by delivering on the American Dream of a better idea: A healthcare professional career-track paradigm that is revolutionary and doable! Imagine the faces of the students at graduation or months and even years later with a big smile when they speak of their incessant curiosity with healthcare and their success.

> The *Exercise Medicine Clinic* is the best idea because it has all of the advantages of being a success, and it is a great idea whose time has come.

It will be something to see and to feel. Students will no longer be frustrated or angry because now they will see themselves as successful in their chosen profession.

As President John F. Kennedy said, "Change is the law of life. And those who only look to the past or present are certain to miss the future." No, it doesn't mean the end to publishing. On the contrary, it is simply a more natural balance between research and teaching that doesn't exist now but will in the future.

Remember, there is nothing wrong with new ideas, different possibilities that have not been tried, and taking the time to do the right things for the right reasons. Remember this simple reality check: If we are not part of the solution, we are the problem. So, why not stand up, think differently, and act today on behalf of the profession of exercise physiology and everyone who is interested in healthcare?

I invite you to join the new ASEP perspective and "come to the edge" and experience the community of exercise physiologists creating the profession of exercise physiology rather than taking away from the quality of its existence. There is no need to fear failure, deny who we are, or worrying about doing anything wrong. Rather, ASEP has opened the door that frees us to be who we believe we are. That is exciting because it gives us more energy to participate in life and to celebrate our presence in helping others live a healthier lifestyle.

References

1 Boone, T. (2016). *ASEP's Exercise Medicine Text for Exercise Physiologists*. Beijing, China: Bentham Science Publishing.
2 Hedges, B. (2007). *Who Stole the American Dream II?* Ichikawa, Japan: Inti Publishing.
3 Boone, T. (2012). *The Business of Exercise Physiology*. Lewiston, NY: The Edwin Mellen Press.

INDEX

academic challenges 1–11, 36, 65, 74, 76, 80, 82, 118, 122, 126–8, 140
accountability 2–4, 7–10, 20, 43, 58, 80, 111, 113, 140–2, 145–6
accreditation 13, 15, 17–18, 24, 28; and ASEP path 137–8, 140–1; and business skills 132; and change 125–6; and destiny 40, 44, 81, 83, 94; and healthcare provision 100, 103, 112–14; and leadership 36, 48, 61; and straight thinking 63–7, 69, 71, 74, 77; and transcending limits 119
adenosine triphosphate (ATP) 87, 94, 104
adipose tissue 91
adjuncts 6, 9, 25, 56, 68–9, 124
administrators 4–7, 14–15, 21, 26, 84; and ASEP path 136, 140; and business skills 132; and change 125; and healthcare provision 98, 100; and leadership 35–6, 48, 54–5, 60; and straight thinking 68
aerobic training 92, 94, 138
Ahrens Exercise Physiology Business 66
AICAR 87
Alzheimer's disease 75
American College of Sports Medicine (ACSM) 16, 32, 46, 74, 120
American Dream 8, 55, 146
American Kinesiology Association (AKA) 2
American Society of Exercise Physiologists (ASEP) 1–5, 8, 24–5, 27–8, 146–7; and academic challenges 10–11; and business skills 131–2, 134–5; and change 125–9; and courage 46–53; and destiny 40–1, 43–5, 79–85, 88, 91, 94, 96; future of 64–76; and healthcare provision 98–103, 109, 111–14; and leadership 31–8, 54, 57–8, 60–1; National Office 98; Newsletter 112–13; path of 136–44; and possibilities 14–19, 139–40; and straight thinking 63–9, 71–7; and transcending limits 116–23
anatomy 35, 39, 43, 67–8, 94
anxiety 60, 85, 88–9, 110, 112, 140
APTA 10
Aristotle 33
Armstrong, N. 52
arteries 91, 93, 95–6, 101, 105, 108
arteriovenous oxygen difference 93, 102, 105
arthritis 3, 103, 112

back pain 3
Beijing Sport University 87
Berger, B. 124–5
Berra, Y. 120
Board Certification 2–4, 15, 17–18, 26, 28; and academic challenges 6, 8, 10; and ASEP path 137–41, 143; and business skills 134–5; and change 126; and courage 48, 52–3; and destiny 42–4, 79–81, 83, 85, 88, 94, 96; and healthcare provision 98, 100–3, 109–15; and leadership 31–4, 61; and straight thinking 65–7, 69, 71–2, 74–6; and transcending limits 117–19
Board of Directors (BOD) 83, 113, 123

body fat 85–6, 88, 101, 116
body weight 94, 105, 110
Bowman Grey School of Medicine 68
Brown, H. J. 83
Buscaglia, L. F. 81
The Business of Exercise Physiology 76
business/business skills 5–6, 24, 35, 65–6, 145–6; and ASEP path 139–40, 143; business management 130–5; business plans 76, 132, 134, 139; and destiny 43, 81, 95; and healthcare provision 100, 109; and straight thinking 69, 73, 76; and transcending limits 119

Callanta, R. 132
Campbell, T. C. 135
Campbell, T. M. 135
cancers 75, 79, 86–8, 90, 103, 112, 114, 134, 138
cardiac output 90–1, 93–4, 96, 102, 104–5, 107–8
cardiorespiratory system 85, 94, 101, 103
cardiovascular disease 3, 84, 87, 91, 110, 114, 138
cardiovascular system 91, 103, 134
careers 2, 5–9, 13–15, 23–9, 146; and ASEP path 137–8, 140; and business skills 130–3; and change 124, 128; and courage 46, 48, 50, 54–6, 59–60; and destiny 40–1, 44–5, 83; and healthcare provision 98–9, 109, 113; and leadership 31–3, 35–8, 59–60; and straight thinking 63–4, 66, 69–71, 74–6; and transcending limits 117–19, 121
Carpenter, L. 22
Carroll, S. 22
cash-based practices 133–4
Chan, P. S. 22
change 116–20, 124–30, 139–43, 147
cholesterol 134
Churchill, W. 139
College of St Scholastica (CSS) 4, 17, 66, 68, 112
college teachers/college teaching 21, 24, 26–7, 29, 145; and academic challenges 1, 4–10; and ASEP path 136–7; and business skills 132–3; and change 124, 127; and courage 50–1; and destiny 42–3, 45, 80; and healthcare provision 99, 114; and leadership 35, 54–61; and possibilities 14–17; and research 69–73; and transcending limits 117–18
coronary heart disease 34, 86, 88, 90–1, 101
courage 15, 19, 36, 46–53, 58, 77, 113, 143
critical thinking 13, 34, 59, 69, 111–12

curricula 18, 24–5, 29, 36, 43–4, 58, 84; and academic challenges 7–8; and ASEP path 138, 140; and business skills 130–2; and courage 51; and healthcare provision 98; and straight thinking 69, 74
cystic fibrosis 103

Darwin, C. 66
debt 5–6, 9, 24, 32, 34, 40, 76, 118, 124
DePree, M. 44
depression 75, 81, 85, 90, 112, 114, 125, 127, 134, 138
destiny 10, 39–45, 47, 53, 72, 79–97, 126
DeVos, R. M. 117
diabetes 3, 18, 79, 84, 90; and ASEP path 138; and business skills 134; and destiny 92, 96; and healthcare provision 103, 110, 112, 114; and leadership 34; and straight thinking 75
diagnoses 101, 103
diastolic blood pressure (DBP) 94, 102, 108
dogma 120–2, 136
D'Orso, M. 136
double product (DP) 85, 93–5, 102, 105
Du Bois, W. E. B. 82

ego 12, 38, 74, 123
electrocardiography (ECG) 101–3
electron transport system (ETS) 94
endothelium 91
entrepreneurship 15–16, 23–6, 42–4, 88, 145; and academic challenges 6, 8, 10; and ASEP path 140, 143; and business management 130–4; and change 117, 119; and healthcare provision 100; and leadership 33, 60–1; and straight thinking 65, 74, 76–7; and vision 125
equations 34, 93–5, 104–9
ergometers 21, 101, 103, 105, 109
Establishment 141–3, 146
ethics 15–17, 24, 26, 28, 146; and academic challenges 2, 4–8; and accountability 140; and ASEP path 139–42; and business skills 133; and change 125; and courage 48–9, 52; and destiny 40, 43, 79, 81, 83–4, 87–8, 94; and healthcare provision 99, 111, 113–14; and leadership 32–3, 38, 58; and straight thinking 64, 68, 71, 74, 76; and transcending limits 116, 119
evaluation 103–4, 113, 140
Evans, R. 87
exercise medicine 14–15, 17–19, 24–5, 29, 145–6; and academic challenges 1–3, 8, 11; and ASEP path 137–41, 143; and business management 130–5; and change

117, 119; and courage 47, 50; and destiny 41, 43–5, 84–91; and dogma 122; and ethics 112; exercise medicine clinics 25, 43, 60, 74, 100, 109, 131, 134, 138, 143, 145–6; and healthcare provision 103–5, 109, 114–15; and leadership 31–2, 34–7, 60; physiology of 92–6; and purpose 126–7; and straight thinking 65–6, 68–9, 71, 74–5; and student dilemmas 100; and vascular perspective 91

Exercise Physiologist Certified (EPC) 2, 17–18, 53, 68, 137–8

Exercise Physiology (EP) 145–7; and academic challenges 1–11; and accreditation 112–13; and analysis 110; and ASEP path 136–44; and business 130–5; and change 124–9; and courage 46–53; and destiny 39–45, 79–97; and ethics 111–12; Exercise Physiology Practice 3, 133–4; and healthcare provision 98–115; and instruction 109–10; and leadership 31–8, 54–62; and physiology of exercise medicine 92–6; and possibilities 12–20; practice of 100–2; and purpose of physiologists 126–7; and research 21–30; and students 21–30; and thinking straight 63–78; and transcending limits 116–23; and treatment 110

exercise pills 84–90

exercise science 13–14, 16, 22–5, 52, 146; and academic challenges 1–2, 5–8; and accountability 140–1; and ASEP path 136–8; and change 118–20, 127–8; and courage 52; and destiny 40–3, 80, 83–4, 94; and leadership 32–3, 35–7; and purpose 126; and straight thinking 63–5, 67, 70–1, 73, 75; and student dilemmas 99; and vision 125

exploitation 60, 68

faculty 13–17, 21–6, 28–9, 50–1, 145; and academic challenges 1–2, 4–10; and ASEP path 136–41; and business skills 130–2; and change 124–5, 127; and courage 50–1; and destiny 41, 44, 80; and healthcare provision 98–100; and leadership 32, 34–6, 56–7, 59, 61; and straight thinking 64, 68–70; and transcending limits 118–20

fee-for-service approach 43

Ferriss, T. 82

Florida State University (FSU) 67

Freeman, L. 68

frequency of breaths (Fb) 92–4

Frost, R. 82

Gandhi, M. 44
GlaxoSmithKline 87
goals 39–42, 47–8, 51, 53, 71, 81, 83, 100–1, 127, 134, 139, 143
Goethe, J. W. von 55
graduate schools 24, 32, 64, 99, 133, 138
grants 21, 56, 69, 71, 100
Great Britain 86, 139
Greenleaf, R. 33
Grossman, S. C. 34
groupthink 5, 7

Harmon, V. 76
Harvard 22, 141
healthcare 12–13, 15–16, 18–19, 24–9, 146–7; and academic challenges 1–5, 8–9; and accreditation 113; and ASEP path 136–41, 143; and business management 130–3, 135; and change 128, 116–17, 119; and courage 46–50, 52–3; and destiny 39–45, 79–80, 83–5, 88, 95; and dogma 121–2; and ethics 111; healthcare provision 98–115; and leadership 31, 33–8, 60–1; and new profession 81–91; and physiology of exercise medicine 92; and purpose 127; and straight thinking 65–9, 71–6; and transcending limits 122; and vision 125–6
heart disease 3, 75, 86–8, 90, 92, 96, 134
heart rate (HR) 90–3, 95–6, 102–3, 105–7
heart weight 94, 106, 108
hemodynamic forces 91–2, 102
Henry, M. 60
Hesburg, T. M. 74
high blood pressure 3, 75, 84, 92, 96
human performance 6–7, 22–3, 41, 63, 73, 137, 141
hypertension 85–6, 90, 103, 134, 138

inflation 5, 65
innovation 26, 29
instruction 109–10
insulin 81, 88, 92, 114
Integrating Spirituality and Exercise Physiology 68–9
integrity 7, 9, 15–16, 41, 49, 54–5, 73, 111, 126, 132–3, 143
Introduction to Exercise Physiology 68, 125

Jacobson, J. 57
Jarman, B. 43
job opportunities 22, 24, 63–4, 98–9, 145–6; and ASEP path 138, 140; and change 124; and employability strategies 6; and healthcare provision 109; and purpose

127; and transcending limits 118–21; and vision 125
Journal of Professional Exercise Physiology (JPEP) 17
journals 15, 17, 21, 24, 26; and change 127; and courage 49; and healthcare provision 112–13; and leadership 56, 59–60; and straight thinking 66, 70, 75

Kanter, R. M. 141
Kendzoir, S. 69
Kennedy, J. F. 147
Kierkegaard, S. 82
kilocalories 104
kinesiology 18, 22–3, 25, 35, 52; and academic challenges 1–2, 6–7; and ASEP path 137, 141; and change 126; and destiny 80, 94; and straight thinking 63–5, 71, 73; and student dilemmas 99; and transcending limits 120; and vision 125
Kipps, C. 3

Laher, I. 87–8
Land, G. 43
leadership 13–16, 19, 32–3, 37–8, 145–6; and academic challenges 2, 9; and accountability 141, 143; and accreditation 113; and ASEP path 63–7, 70–1, 73–4, 137, 139–40, 143; and change 117, 119–20, 128; and courage 49, 52–3; and destiny 41, 43–4, 80, 82, 88, 92; and disconnect 131; and ethics 112; failure of leadership 4–9; and healthcare provision 114; new leadership 31–8; and purpose 127; and search for leaders 54–62; and transcending limits 122–3; and vision 126
left ventricular power output (LVPO) 107–8
Li, S. 87–8
licensure 12, 80, 103, 137, 141
Ligand Pharmaceuticals 87
lipid levels 81, 90, 103, 114
loans 9, 13–14, 23–5, 34, 63, 130

Malcolm X 141
malpractice suits 43
Marguleas, H. 128
marketing 4, 76, 139
May, R. 47, 52
mean arterial pressure (MAP) 102, 108
measurement 103–4
medical schools 64, 68–9, 118
mediocrity 9, 27, 34, 38, 42, 118, 127, 139, 141
mentoring 8
metabolic syndrome 90, 92

metabolism 3, 13, 18, 21, 34–5, 67, 71, 85–7, 94, 101–4, 109–10
Midwestern State University 83
Millman, D. 72
mortality 66, 75, 91
motivation 10, 15, 33, 66, 81, 116, 134, 143
Munroe, M. 126
muscle function 18, 92
musculoskeletal disabilities 3, 131
musculoskeletal system 85, 92, 101, 103, 110
myocardial infarction 87, 95, 102
myocardial oxygen consumption 85, 93–5, 102, 105–7

Narkar, V. A. 87
Nightingale, E. 116
Northwestern State University (NSU) 39, 67

Oaklander, M. 81
obesity 3, 18, 85–6, 90, 92, 103, 112, 114, 134, 138
Official Credo 49
organ transplants 103
osteoarthritis 3, 112
osteoporosis 112, 114
Overstreet, H. A. 82
oxygen 13, 81, 85, 90, 92–5, 102, 104–7, 109

paradigm shifts 46, 141, 145–6
parents 15, 22–4, 26–7, 39, 41; and academic challenges 4–7, 9–10; and ASEP path 140; and business skills 130; and change 124; and healthcare provision 99; and leadership 32, 34, 57–9; and straight thinking 65, 71, 76; and transcending limits 118–20
partnerships 133
Paulson, S. 83
pedagogy 25
perfection 39–40
peripheral vascular disease 103
personal trainers 3, 8, 18, 25, 31; and change 126; and destiny 82, 84, 92–5; and healthcare provision 98–9; and leadership 37; and straight thinking 64, 72–4; and transcending limits 120
pharmaceutical industry 87, 89
phenotypes 91
Phillips, B. 136
physiology 5, 92–6
plaque 91

possibilities 12–20, 29, 48, 66, 72, 83, 116–17, 129, 139–40, 143, 147
pre-professional degrees 64, 71–2
Presbyterians 60
prescription 18, 34, 36–7, 43, 69; and ASEP path 137, 139; and business management 130; and change 117; and ethics 112; and exercise medicine 79, 84–6, 88, 90, 96; and healthcare provision 104, 110, 114–15; and purpose 126; and straight thinking 75
professional development 5, 16, 19, 27–8, 43; and accreditation 112; and ASEP path 139; and courage 46, 50; and healthcare provision 114; and leadership 32–3, 54; and straight thinking 71
professional organizations 13, 16, 19–20, 26–8, 146; and academic challenges 10–11; and ASEP path 137–40, 142–3; and business management 135; and change 117, 119, 128–9; and courage 46–8, 51–2; and destiny 41–2, 44–5; and dogma 121–2; and exercise medicine 80, 82–3, 88; and future of ASEP 64–76; and healthcare provision 114; and leadership 31–8, 55, 57; and purpose 126–7; and straight thinking 63, 70, 72–4, 76; and transcending limits 116, 123; and vision 125
professionalism 13–17, 19, 24, 26–9, 145–6; and academic challenges 5–8, 10; and accreditation 112–13; and ASEP path 139; and business management 132–3; and change 117, 119, 124, 128; commitment to 35–7; and courage 46–7, 49, 52; and destiny 43–4; and exercise medicine 79–80, 88; and healthcare provision 99, 114; and leadership 33, 54, 58; and straight thinking 66, 71–2
professionalization 14, 16–17, 31, 41, 75; and academic challenges 11; and accreditation 113; and ASEP path 137; and change 119, 128; and exercise medicine 81–2; and purpose 127; and transcending limits 122
Professionalization of Exercise Physiology-online (PEPonline) 17, 49, 75
profit 24, 46, 89, 133
Prozac 75
public sector 3, 23, 26, 35, 60, 63, 75, 81, 86, 92, 117, 119
pulmonary diseases 103, 110

Rawlings, H. R. 41
Reagan, R. 141

regression equations 34, 93, 102, 104, 107
research 13–17, 19, 40–3, 45–6, 145–7; and academic challenges 1–2, 4–5, 8–9; and accreditation 112; and ASEP path 136–40; and business management 133, 135; and change 117, 124; and college teachers 69–73; and courage 48, 50, 52; and disconnect 131; and dogma 120–1; and ethics 111–12; and exercise medicine 79–80, 84, 87–8; and healthcare provision 98, 114; and leadership 31–6, 54–7, 59–61; and purpose 126; and straight thinking 65; and students 21–30, 99–100; and vision 125–6
resistance training 92, 110
responsibilities 14–15, 21, 36, 54, 57–60; and ASEP path 136, 142; and business management 132; and change 117, 125, 128; and destiny 41–2, 79–80; and dogma 121; and ethics 111; and healthcare provision 101–2, 115; and purpose 126; and straight thinking 66, 68, 72, 76–7; and student dilemmas 100; and transcending limits 116
Robbins, T. 67
Roosevelt, T. 118

Salk Institute 87
sarcopenia 87
Schuller, R. A. 38, 51
sedentary lifestyles 76, 86–9, 92, 96, 114
Shinn, F. S. 49
skeletal muscles 91–4, 103
spirituality 34, 66, 68–9
sports medicine 16–17, 36, 41, 43–4, 50, 52, 84, 120, 127–8, 136, 146
sports sciences 7, 23, 63, 73, 125, 137
standards 17, 24, 28, 40, 146; and academic challenges 2–6, 8; and ASEP path 137–8; and business skills 131; and change 125; and courage 48–9, 52; and destiny 43; and exercise medicine 81, 84; and healthcare provision 111, 113–14; and leadership 31, 58, 61; and straight thinking 71, 73–4; and transcending limits 122
status quo 13, 17, 27, 46–8, 146; and academic challenges 2, 5, 7; and ASEP path 138, 141–2; and business skills 135; and change 125, 128; and courage 52; and exercise medicine 83; and leadership 33–4, 37–8, 54–5, 57; and straight thinking 70, 72; and transcending limits 118, 120, 122
Steele, S. 76

straight thinking 63–78, 122
stress 1, 66, 76, 84, 88–9, 91, 103, 110, 133, 140
stroke 34, 75, 86–7, 90–1
stroke volume (SV) 90–6, 102, 105, 107
Sugarman, D. A. 68
superoxide dismutase 91
systemic vascular resistance (SVR) 102, 108–9
systolic blood pressure (SBP) 93, 95, 102, 105–8

taxation 134
tenure 6, 14–16, 22–3, 25–6, 40, 42, 54, 59, 69, 117–18
textbooks 16, 21, 68, 125
tidal volume 92–3
tissue extraction 93, 102, 105
titles 79–81
total peripheral resistance (TPR) 108
tuition fees 4–7, 13–14, 23–5, 32, 42, 59, 61, 65, 73, 76, 124, 146
tuition loans 9, 13–14, 23–5, 34, 63, 130
type 2 diabetes mellitus 3, 18, 75, 79, 90, 92, 114, 134, 138

unemployment 4, 8–9, 25, 40, 50, 64
United States (US) 32, 34, 42, 50, 52; and academic challenges 3–4, 6–7; and accreditation 113; Bureau of Labor Statistics 75; and business management 134; and change 117, 119; and exercise medicine 81, 85–6, 88–9; and healthcare provision 98, 104; and straight thinking 63, 66, 68–9; and students 23, 100

University of British Columbia 87
University of Florida 67
University of Louisiana 67, 124
University of Mississippi Medical School 68
University of Southampton 86
University of Southern Mississippi (USM) 68

Valiga, T. M. 34
Van de Ven, A. 120
vascular cells 91–2
vasodilation 91
ventilation 92–3
ventricles 91–2, 94, 102, 106–8
Vernon Parish Library 67
vision 19, 22, 39, 41–2, 44–5; and academic challenges 5, 8; and accountability 142; and accreditation 113; and ASEP path 137, 139, 143; and change 128–9; and courage 47–9, 53; and dogma 121–2; and exercise medicine 79–81, 84; and healthcare provision 114; and leadership 31, 34, 37, 54–5, 57; power of 125–6; and purpose 127; and straight thinking 70–1, 74; and students 28, 100; and transcending limits 116, 123
Vivekananda, S. 53

Wake Forest University (WFU) 67–8
Wattles, M. 75
Weissmann, J. 100
World Anti-Doping Agency (WADA) 87
Wyatt, F. 83